CONFESSIONS OF
A KOSHER MEDIUM

Spirits, Scandal and Sparkly Shoes

BEV MANN
with Linda Dearsley

First published in paperback by
Michael Terence Publishing in 2021
www.mtp.agency

Copyright © 2021 Bev Mann

Bev Mann has asserted the right to be identified as the author of this work in accordance with the Copyright, Designs and Patents Act 1988

ISBN 9781800942103

No part of this publication may be reproduced, stored in a retrieval system, or transmitted, in any form or by any means, electronic, mechanical, photocopying, recording or otherwise, without the prior permission of the publishers

Cover image by Mikaela Morgan

Cover background
Copyright © Nikki Zalewski
www.123rf.com

*To my Mum, my Dad and all my friends
in the Spirit World*

> "There are more things in Heaven and Earth than are dreamt of…"
>
> — Shakespeare

CONTENTS:

ONE:
'Mummy I want to tell you a story...' 9

TWO:
The Taps turned as if by magic... 19

THREE:
Wait till your mother gets home... 29

FOUR:
'Where are you in the room, Spirit?' asked Jilly. 45

FIVE:
'We can't help... this is your Dad's time...' 55

SIX:
'You should be doing this,' said the Medium... 80

SEVEN:
'You've just described my dead husband...' 97

EIGHT:
A big, dark shadow of a man shot through the window into the room... 113

NINE:
'Every time she speaks, I see sparkles flying around...' 129

TEN:
What me stand on stage? That wasn't
going to happen ever...   143

ELEVEN:
'Your feet aren't going to touch the
ground...' he said.   161

TWELVE:
The woman said, 'I want to stick pins
in my husband's eyes...'   177

THIRTEEN:
How lovely to live in a house touched
by angels...   193

FOURTEEN:
Sparkly boots featured in every
window... it was destiny!   201

FIFTEEN:
Right by my foot was the little
golden heart...   214

SIXTEEN:
The view was bathed in a peaceful,
angelic light...   227

PS:
Hello there!   231

PPS:
Oh and finally, before I go...   235

MEET THE AUTHOR: 239

ONE:

'Mummy I want to tell you a story…'

There was no doubt about it, Mum wasn't in a rush to go. After battling a long, debilitating illness we had to accept that at the age of ninety-three, she'd finally reached the end of the road. She'd been unconscious for almost a week, my sister Lorraine and I at her bedside.

'She can't possibly last the night,' the nurse warned us, evening after evening and yet somehow, she always did. It was almost as if she was hovering between two worlds. Neither here nor there.

It was heart-breaking. But what am I doing just sitting here? I thought suddenly that night, wiping away another useless tear. I'm a medium. Surely I can find out what's going on. We'd already tried everything to ease her path. We'd given her permission to go, we'd left the room and come back but still Mum hung on. I shut my eyes. Lorraine probably thought I was having a nap – we were both exhausted after all. But behind my closed eyelids I was actually willing myself to connect. I needed to relax, free my mind and reach out psychically. Gradually my breathing slowed, the tension in my shoulders eased and the sounds of the sick-room faded away. It became very quiet, very still.

Then all at once, I could hear music playing and the tang of cigarette smoke tickled my nose. I seemed to be in some sort of cabin, decked out like a sophisticated cocktail bar. There was soft lighting, a glamorous, retro '50's look and from somewhere, an unseen saxophonist was wafting lazy melodies into the crowded room. There was clearly a party going on. All around, people were lounging across velvet chairs, laughing and joking, sipping drinks, clinking glasses and happily smoking cigarettes indoors without a care – just like they did in those days.

Then I did a double take. I knew these people. They were my relatives - long passed. There was my Dad over there, glass in one hand, beckoning me over with the other, a big smile on his face. And the others – all from Mum's side of the family. Aunts and uncles and even dear old Grandpa Maurie, all laughing and chatting, clearly enjoying themselves.

'I know, I know,' said Dad, when I reached him, as if reading my mind, 'I'm here waiting for Mum, whenever she's ready.'

'But Dad,' I replied in my head, kind of telling him off, 'She's ready to go. Can you hurry up? Stop partying and come for her!'

But suddenly he was looking past me. I glanced round to see what had caught his eye and almost gasped. There in the doorway stood Mummy, but younger and slimmer than I'd ever seen her. She was wearing a stunning white dress, nipped in at her tiny waist, her shining auburn hair was curled around her face and she was holding a cigarette in a cigarette holder in her hand. Wow! She was so beautiful. Like a movie star.

Dad's face lit up. They'd never stopped adoring each other and now he moved eagerly forward to make a fuss of her. I opened my eyes a chink. There, back in the sombre sick room my sister Lorraine was still holding Mum's hand and Mum was still there. Pale, desperately thin and unresponsive, but still there.

I shut my eyes again. 'Well Dad, what's going on? Mummy's still lying here and she needs you to come to her.'

'I know,' said Dad. 'The trouble is it's the father's job to come and collect his daughter. I've got to wait.'

I looked around for Papa Maurie. 'Well Papa,' I said, 'when are you coming for Mummy?'

'I'm having trouble reaching her,' said my grandfather apologetically. He waved his arm by way of explanation and another scene opened up before me. I was looking down on a vast expanse of watery mud and standing there, feet stuck in the thick sludge was Mummy. Every time she tried to lift her leg to move forward it was like she was glued to the ground. I could see Papa trying to stretch down from the clouds to help her but he just couldn't reach.

Poor Mummy was trying so hard. 'Can't the family help?' I asked Papa.

'Let's see,' said Papa. He called the family together and as I watched, they gathered round and Grandma Sarah, Mum's Mum, my two uncles, my aunt and my Dad linked hands to form a family chain-ladder to try to reach down to Mum.

I opened my eyes. Back in the sick-room it was now officially Sedar night – the very special night before Passover – the Jewish festival – that had always been so important to

Mummy. So my sister and I fetched the silver candlesticks Mum and Dad had treasured since their wedding day and we took it in turns to light the candles.

'Look Mummy,' said Lorraine, heading back to the bedside. 'We've lit the candles. It's Sedar Night.'

And though she'd been in a coma for almost a week, I'll swear Mum nodded her head as if she'd heard.

I sat down beside Lorraine. 'Mummy I want to tell you a story of what I've just seen in my meditation,' I said. Lorraine might think I'd gone crazy but somehow it seemed really important Mum knew the details of my vision.

So I proceeded to recount the whole experience: how I'd seen her stuck fast in gooey mud while Dad and all the family were sitting round having a good time waiting for her to join them and how she'd suddenly appeared, looking so beautiful and slender in this glorious white dress. 'Oh Mum,' I said, 'See how amazing you look. Look at your tiny waist. And now, right now at this minute, they're all waiting for you to join them at their Passover table.'

Maybe it was fanciful but as I spoke I got the feeling Mum was listening, listening with great intensity, hanging onto every word. When I finally finished there was a long pause. The room went very silent, almost as if we were all waiting. Then suddenly, Mummy's eyes flew open really wide. She was staring transfixed at someone or something at the end of the bed – quite invisible to us.

'Look, they're all here for you,' I said quickly, though I couldn't actually see them myself. 'Can you see Daddy and your mummy and daddy? And there's your sister Shirley and your brothers. Go to them. Go to the light. It's ok to go.'

And as we watched, her eyes grew wider – she took a deep breath, then all at once, she was gone. It was 9.03pm. The strange thing was, almost before our eyes, her face relaxed and rearranged itself. The poor, careworn features smoothed, became tranquil and somehow appeared at least 30 years younger. It was as if three decades and months of illness just fell away, and there she was, young, serene and beautiful the way she was meant to be.

In the midst of our sadness, Lorraine and I were awestruck. It felt like a kind of miracle.

People often say when you're bereaved, it must be wonderfully lucky to be a bereaved medium: 'Because then you can talk to your loved ones, or even see them, whenever you want!' But I have to explain that unfortunately it doesn't work quite like that. I only wish it did!

Maybe it's because if you could call up your own late relatives and friends for a chat any time you fancied, you'd spend so long catching up with them you wouldn't get round to using your gift for what it's intended – putting *other* people in touch with *their* loved ones.

Sometimes, it's true. If they have something really important to let us mediums know, our loved ones do spontaneously get a message through, but more often a medium will have to visit another medium if he or she wants to contact her own loved ones.

'But it must be so comforting to believe. To know they're

safe somewhere, waiting for you. There's no reason to be sad.' That's another thing people say.

And of course that's true too. It *is* comforting. Yet like everyone else, we still miss the physical presence of the much-loved person who's moved on. How we long for the sound of that familiar voice, the warm hug, the cherished features – so of course mediums end up grieving, just like everyone else.

Which is how it was that even though I knew Mum was probably partying up there with Dad and the rest of her family, perfectly happy and looking down on us every now and then, I still missed her dreadfully.

Yes, it's an odd thing being a medium. I didn't grow up knowing I was a medium of course. It took me years to find out. I only knew I seemed to be a bit different. I didn't quite fit in anywhere.

I was very quiet and shy as a child and my parents were perplexed because I often woke up in the night screaming.

They thought I had 'night terrors' – which I did in a way but not in the way they thought. I'd wake up in the darkness and see lights floating round my bed. I'd watch them for a while, quite fascinated as they bobbed about, but then they'd move in closer and closer until I could see there were faces inside those glowing globes, human faces and next thing I knew I was screaming for Mum and Dad.

Once when I was about 5 years old we were on holiday in Cliftonville on the Kent, coast staying at the traditional family hotel my parents took us to every year. Somehow, one afternoon I managed to get lost. I think I must have gone up to our room on my own and was coming back down to rejoin Mum and Dad and Lorraine in the lounge, when suddenly everything looked unfamiliar.

I must have turned the wrong way down the corridor and gone down a different staircase or something but suddenly there in front of me on the stairs was a strange man. He was all dressed up like a court jester from Tudor times. He had a funny hat on his head like a soft crown with bells on and he was wearing a brightly coloured tunic, clashing tights and odd, long thin shoes.

He turned and saw me standing there, open-mouthed with shock. I can't say that he did anything wrong, or threatening but for some reason the very sight of him was terrifying. Looking back, I'm sure he was a spirit person but as a small child all I knew was there was something not right about him. He didn't belong - in a strange way I couldn't understand, so once again, I was off and running in a panic to find my Mum and Dad.

They searched the hotel of course but could find no entertainer or costumed performer of any kind on the premises. In the end they put the incident down to my overactive imagination.

Yet despite so many frights I never came to any actual harm. In fact it was almost as if I was being protected. On one occasion, on yet another holiday I reckon I almost met my guardian angel.

I think it must have been a rainy summer because some time

after our Cliftonville break my hard-working parents decided to treat us to two weeks of sunshine in Italy, at a resort near Rimini.

We were coming out of our hotel one evening, Mum, Dad, Lorraine and I, intending to make for a nearby restaurant, when for some reason, without waiting for them, I just stepped off the pavement and daydreamed straight out into the road – right into the path of a speeding car.

Horrified screams split the street. There was a terrible screeching of brakes and suddenly big hands grabbed my shoulders, I was being yanked violently upwards and backwards through the air to land unsteadily back beside my mother on the pavement. I was absolutely fine, if baffled, but Mum was crying and Dad, who'd somehow sprung forward and managed to drag me to safety, was trembling from head to foot. Behind them, a group of other guests who'd emerged at the same time as us seemed to be dabbing away tears too.

Well-meaning passers-by ran over to pat me down and check for broken bones and there was much hugging and animated chattering over my head in a language I didn't understand. What all the fuss was about I couldn't imagine but it seemed my almost certain death, had been witnessed by dozens of shocked tourists.

Mum told me when I was older it was a miracle the car didn't hit me that night. In fact how it managed to stop in time, and how Dad was able to leap from the pavement and snatch me from the jaws of death in a fraction of a second, she was still unable to understand.

'We couldn't see how it could possibly miss you,' said Mum. 'Yet it did.'

I didn't understand at the time of course but now I think my guardian angel was working overtime that night. The spirit world obviously didn't want me back just yet. There were other plans for my future.

TWO:

The Taps turned as if by magic...

It was Simon, my soon to-be-future-husband who pointed it out. There we were, Simon, Mum, Dad, Lorraine and me all sitting round in the best room – the front room of our semi in Edgware, north west London – about to have the traditional Friday night dinner together.

To be honest that front room, which was actually two rooms knocked into one was a bit of a mausoleum. It was only ever used for 'best'. The rest of the time Mum, Dad, Lorraine and I lived in the cosy little extension at the back that overlooked the garden. The Morning Room as Mum called it.

Anyway Simon took one look at the dining-room chair offered to him that evening and clearly had some sort of rush of blood to the head. 'Well we don't want to be sitting on plastic forever!' he said suddenly, and with that he lunged forward and ripped off the yellowing polythene that had covered Mum's pristine upholstered seat since the day it had been delivered – years before. So many years in fact, that the rest of us no longer even noticed.

There was a shocked, horrified silence. We stared at the exposed cushion, quite stunned.

Then we all looked at each other and burst out laughing. Well, apart from Mum who was not sure she saw the funny side. The next minute, still giggling a shade hysterically, we were all ripping the plastic from our own seats to reveal the spotless, untouched fabric beneath.

Unfortunately, the naked cushions in their unfaded glory still failed to make the chairs look new. Over years of use, the upholstery had sagged out of shape and now, without their plastic 'corsets', the seats just slumped, brighter, but exhausted-looking. Still, they were much less crackly to sit on.

Mum reluctantly admitted that yes, they were more comfortable now. And more colourful. All the same, she drew the line at any further liberation of household textiles. The plastic runner over the carpet in the hall was here to stay. Future son-in-law or not there were only so many liberties she'd tolerate from Simon.

Although we teased Mum now and then about these little things though, we did understand she worked very hard to provide us with a good home. She just had different ideas about how to keep it that way.

We were a small but very close family. The four of us were quite content in our three-bedroom semi. We'd moved there when I was about 18 months old and it was the only home I could remember. There was a square bay window at the front and a pretty garden at the back. Mum and Dad weren't gardeners but there was a patch of grass with a circular paved area in the middle, an old apple tree at the end and flower beds full of roses. And of course this being the '70s there was a lot of orange carpet marching through the house and boldly patterned floral wallpaper enlivened most rooms.

Mum and Dad both worked in the family ladies-wear shop - a tiny little establishment not much bigger than a market stall in an arcade in Brixton, South London, close to Brixton market. We called it the Hole in the Wall. Dad had called the shop 'Leonard's' after his father who'd encouraged him in setting up the venture. So every morning Mum and Dad would climb into Dad's Ford Cortina for the long journey through the crawling traffic from one side of the London to the other. They'd spend the whole day working at the shop, then they'd take the slow drive home again, whereupon Mum would throw off her coat and launch straight into cooking a full scale, meat and two veg family meal. Mum never seemed to stop working.

On Sundays they were off again – heading for the East End and the wholesalers to buy new stock for the coming week. Quite often Lorraine and I would go with them. It was either that or Cheder – the Jewish Sunday School. Lorraine never wanted to go to Cheder and if she wasn't going, neither was I. I liked to do what my big sister did.

Besides, those wholesale clothing factories were like a fascinating, other world. They weren't really supposed to be for family parties but if Lorraine and I kept very quiet and made sure not to draw attention to ourselves we could peep in. I stared in wonder at the noisy rooms full of whirring sewing machines, bales of cloth and nimble-fingered women bent over billowing fabric that flew expertly through the chattering needles.

Then there'd be the showrooms, crammed with racks of garments in polythene sleeves. Mum and Dad would spend ages skimming through the hangers, sliding them back and forth, trying to decide which items and sizes would appeal most to next week's customers.

This could get a bit boring but Lorraine and I shuffled from foot to foot impatiently willing them on - because the best bit of the day came afterwards. As soon as Mum and Dad had decided on their selections, big heaps of garments were carefully laid in the boot and then we were off to Blooms – the famous Kosher restaurant in Whitechapel for a slap-up traditional Jewish lunch.

Blooms had been going for years and years. There were always queues outside and when you got in, there were these funny double seats to sit on to eat chicken soup, salt beef sandwiches, latkas – a type of potato pancake – and chopped liver. Strangely enough, all the waiters seemed to be Mediterranean for some reason and in a terrible hurry, but Dad was so friendly and made a point of getting to know them by name and we were always made welcome.

Outside the restaurant there was always an old Jewish lady dressed in an old fashioned long skirt, headscarf and little ankle boots selling fresh bagels. She seemed to be as much of a fixture as the restaurant itself, in fact I believe she became quite famous. So of course, despite being full of food we'd usually end up buying a bag of bagels to take home as well.

Back in Edgware, Lorraine and I rounded off the outing with an evening spent helping Mum and Dad mark up the stock for the next day. We'd write the size of each new item and its price on a little white ticket tied to a piece of string, then carefully thread the string through the zip of each garment. By bedtime there'd be a big stack of neatly labelled clothes all ready to be hung on the rails at the family shop next morning.

Looking back, I can see we were quite a team.

Mum and Dad's busiest day was Saturday of course, so when we were very young, they had an au pair to look after us while they were at work.

Most of the au pairs were lovely girls. Mainly from Denmark and Sweden, they were eager to improve their English and happy to put up with Lorraine and I, even when we squabbled. We became so fond of many of them we became pen friends after they left and carried on exchanging letters with them for years.

But when I was still quite small there was one we just didn't take to. I'm not sure why I didn't like her. She was aloof, spent most of the time in her room and paid little attention to Lorraine and I – but it was more than that. There was something about her that frightened me.

Anyway, towards evening this particular Saturday she suddenly decided to give me a bath. Maybe Mum had told her she wanted to find me bathed and put in my pyjamas by the time she got home from work – I don't know. But whatever the reason, this girl seemed to resent it.

I was playing on my own in the bedroom when she unexpectedly appeared. 'It's time for your bath,' she said glowering fiercely. She didn't like me either, that's for sure. Then she stalked into the bathroom, slammed the plug in the tub and turned on the taps. 'Come here!'

That did it. I wasn't going to go to her. Her irritable tone scared me. Before she realised what was happening, I scurried past the bathroom, scampered downstairs and hid behind the sofa in the best room. The au pair shouted some more but I took no notice. Squeezed between the sofa and the wall I heard her angry feet clomping down the stairs.

'Beverley! Beverley!' she shouted. 'Come here, now!'

I made out the sound of the door to the Morning Room squeaking open. Good. She wouldn't find me there! So I leapt out from behind the sofa, raced back upstairs, dashed into the bathroom, slammed the door and locked it. It was an old house and there was still a key operated lock in the bathroom.

Safe at last! Rather pleased with myself I scrambled onto the loo-seat and put my fingers in my ears as the au pair charged back up the stairs and began rattling the door.

I ignored her furious shouting, kept my ears firmly covered and began swinging my legs and singing a little song to myself. After a while she obviously got sick of me. 'Alright. Stay there then!' she spat and stormed off to her room.

Triumphant, I slid down off the loo-seat. I'd escaped her clutches. Hurrah! That's when I noticed hot water was still pouring into the tub and it was looking rather full. I leaned over to try to turn off the taps but my arms weren't quite long enough.

'Beverley! Beverley! She's gone. You can come out now,' it

was Lorraine's voice outside. 'Come on. Open the door.'

I went to the door, stood on tiptoes and tried to turn the key. It wouldn't budge. I tried again, stretching as tall as I could. Strange. It had turned so easily when I came in but now it wouldn't turn back the other way.

'I can't,' I whispered to Lorraine through the door. 'It's stuck.'

'Stop messing about,' said Lorraine's muffled voice. 'Come on, open the door.'

'I'm not messing about!' I tried the key again. It refused to move. I rattled the handle and shook the door but it was no use. The door stayed firmly locked.

'It won't turn Lorraine!' I cried, beginning to panic. 'It's stuck.'

Lorraine rattled the door and then she kicked it but of course nothing happened.

Then I realised the room was filling with steam and when I looked back at the bath, water was getting close to the rim.

'The bath's nearly overflowing now!' I screamed.

'I'm going to phone Mum!' shouted Lorraine and I heard her run down the stairs.

I began to imagine the hot water spilling over onto the floor and soaking my fluffy slippers and I was trapped. I began to cry.

'It's alright,' said a soft voice near my ear. 'You'll be out soon.'

I looked round. There was no one there.

'Don't worry,' it went on, 'Not long now. Turn off the water.'

I still couldn't see anyone but there was something very soothing about that voice. I wasn't on my own. I felt myself gently guided towards the tub, as if light hands steered my shoulders. Then my arms were lifting over the edge of the bath and this time the taps seemed to be nearer. My fingertips brushed the slippery chrome, the taps turned, and as if by magic, the water stopped.

'Now just sit there and wait,' said the voice. 'Your Mum and Dad are on their way home.'

So I went back to my perch on the loo seat.

After a while I heard the front door open and a multitude of adult feet came crashing up the stairs.

'It's alright Beverley!' cried Dad's voice, 'We'll soon get you out of there.'

And there was a great thud as he hurled himself against the door. The door shuddered but nothing happened. He tried again. There was a horrible, splintering, cracking sound but the door remained obstinately shut.

'Beverley…' called Mum, 'Now don't worry. The fire brigade's here. They're going to break the door down.'

There was another great crash, then another. Everything shook but still the door refused to yield. They certainly made sturdy doors in those days. I sat there watching the wood ripple and vibrate.

'Beverley,' came a deep, unfamiliar voice after several enormous crashes, 'My name's Bill. I'm a fireman. Can you tell me Beverley…is there a key in the lock?'

'Yes,' I said, 'But it won't turn.'

'That's ok Beverley. What I'd like you to do is just take the key out of the lock and see if you can push it under the door…Can you do that?'

I stretched up tall and pulled the key as hard as I could. It toppled out into my hand. Then I knelt down, put it on the floor and pressed it under the crack. I gave a little push and suddenly it disappeared. A couple of seconds later I heard a click, the handle turned and suddenly the door was bursting open. There, framed in the doorway stood a huge fireman in a dark uniform with shiny buttons all down the front.

But it was his face that caught my attention. It seemed to glow with golden light – like it was surrounded by a hazy radiance. Very warm and friendly. In fact as I looked, his whole body seemed to be outlined in sunshine.

I stared at him in fascination. I knew nothing about auras back then of course. How we're all surrounded by our own energy fields that reveal our inner state to those that can see them. All I knew was that this was a very good man. I liked him.

He smiled kindly. 'There you are little lady. Safe and sound now.' He handed the key to Dad. 'I should leave that somewhere else if I were you, sir!'

And then he was off down the stairs and Mum was folding

me in a big hug.

Throughout the whole drama, the au pair remained in her room. She left the next day.

THREE:
Wait till your mother gets home…

I couldn't sleep. It wasn't that late. I could still hear the drone of the TV drifting up the stairs from the living-room, so Mum and Dad were still up. In the next bed though, Lorraine was peacefully dreaming, the blankets pulled up round her ears, only the top of her head visible on the pillow. No point in trying to have a chat with her.

I squeezed my eyes shut, yet the more I tried to get back to sleep, the more awake I became. In the end I slid out of bed, scooped up an armful of toys and took them out to my favourite spot, the little patch of carpet just outside our bedroom door.

It was a good place to play. The landing light made it easy to see and the sounds from downstairs were comforting. And of course I wasn't really on my own. As usual, it wasn't long before the unseen gang arrived to join me.

Strange the way children tend to accept things without asking questions. I didn't know who my playmates were, how many of them there were or even what they looked like. I never saw them.

Yet I could feel them moving around me, I could hear their soft laughter and whispered comments and I just knew what they wanted to play with. Quite often they wanted to play with the same toy as me – which was irritating.

This particular night I was brushing my favourite doll's long, lustrous hair and sorting out the shoes I wanted her to wear, when one of the other little girls tried to tug her out of my hand. I pulled my doll back and held her against my chest. Then I realised the unseen girl was reaching for one of my other dolls. So I grabbed that one as well. Soon I was hoarding piles of teddies and soft animals on my lap as well as the dolls. I was aware of disappointed scuffling amongst the children and small fingers trying to prise a few stragglers out of the heap.

Stubbornly I clung on to my treasures. I wanted them all!

'Get your own toys!' I told them, quite reasonably I thought.

Then all at once that soft voice was in my ear again. The same gentle voice that spoke to me in the bathroom. 'You have to learn to share Beverley,' it said. 'You don't need to play with *all* those things. There's enough for everybody. Share!'

Huh. They're mine! I thought. But the voice persisted. 'It's important to share.' Eventually I relented. Grudgingly I put a few teddies back on the carpet and they were instantly swooped on.

Yet of course it was the doll I really wanted. So bit by bit, the other toys ended up on the carpet too – I was getting tired of hanging onto them anyway. Soon we were playing amicably together again, until my eyelids grew heavy and I gathered everything up and crawled back to bed.

I never thought to wonder who that voice belonged to. Children get so used to adult voices telling them what to do and what not to do, I suppose it just seemed normal.

Now of course I suspect the speaker was probably my guide. We all have a spirit guide, assigned to us even before birth, to help direct us onto the right path as we make our way through the complications of life down here. Even if you can't see or hear your guide you'll be aware of those gut feelings – it's called intuition, an inner knowing.

Back then of course I had no idea what was going on, but my patient guide was obviously close at hand to give me a little nudge from time to time.

Having a guide nearby didn't prevent me from getting up to mischief though. As we grew older and more capable, Lorraine and I began to spend our Saturdays cleaning the house from top to toe for Mum while she was at work. We hoovered and dusted and polished the bathroom till it shone. Then later when Lorraine got a Saturday job, it was just me.

We didn't mind helping out, and the great thing about having the house to ourselves for the day was that we got custody of the phone. It's difficult to imagine now but back then, long before everyone had a mobile, decades before mobiles were even dreamed of, the household phone –shared by all the family members - was still a bit of a novelty. It seems weird now, having to take turns at making a call, but back then being able to chat to your friends, from the comfort of your own hallway was a great treat. Unfortunately, it also caused endless rows in many a home. Teenagers monopolising the line for hours on end, blocking all other calls were a constant source of friction, as were the huge bills that would arrive a few weeks later – no unlimited call deals in those days – for the horrified householder to pay.

Lorraine and I must have made rather free with the phone on Saturdays because after a while Mum and Dad had a lock put on it – effectively barring us from making calls. I'm not sure how the lock was achieved but the end result was when you dialled the numbers, nothing happened, unless you'd tapped in the digits 9… 9 …9 in which case you were allowed to speak to the Emergency services.

This had the effect of spoiling our fun for quite a while since neither of us dared pester the police or the fire brigade. I expect Dad's phone bill became much more manageable too. But then one day I was explaining to a friend why I couldn't phone her after school or even on Saturday – she'd have to phone me - when she came back with some astounding news. She'd not only heard of phone locks – she knew how to unlock them! It was a complicated procedure involving tapping each key the same number of times as the number printed on the key, apparently.

I was thrilled and I was dying to try it out but I had to wait till Saturday. No school of course but I was up early that morning and could hardly contain my impatience as Mum and Dad dawdled over their cuppas and loaded up the car with agonising slowness – or so it seemed to me. But at last they were safely on their way to Brixton. I dashed to the phone and began experimenting, as Lorraine watched with interest. It didn't take long to crack the code. Sure enough, if I tapped the 1 button once and the 2 button twice and so on, I could actually get the phone to ring a proper number. We were thrilled. We resumed our secret Saturday calls on the spot.

We might have carried on like that for months – at least until the next phone bill – had I not made a stupid mistake. Bored and a bit lonely one Saturday when Lorraine had gone out, I decided to have a chat with Mum at work – and let her see how clever I'd been. I happily dialled the shop number and catching Mum in a quiet moment, had a nice long conversation.

Eventually a customer came in. 'Must go,' said Mum and she was just about to put the phone down when an odd thought struck her, 'Where are you phoning me from Beverley?'

'Home of course!' I said smugly.

There was a long silence as the awful truth dawned. 'Beverley!' said Mum sternly, 'Just you wait! Just you wait till I get home!'

I was a bit scared of course but not seriously. Mum was used to the mischief Lorraine and I got up to while she was out and there was always something. To be fair we did our chores like model daughters. But during the long hours when we were unsupervised and left to our own devices - well all sorts of mayhem would break out.

Quite a bit of it involved Lorraine, being the older sister, experimenting with a willing me. One day she was playing at being a nurse so of course I was her patient and she fed me some 'medicine' which she happened to find in Mum's bathroom cabinet. Fortunately, it didn't do any lasting harm but I was pretty sleepy for the next few hours.

Then there was her 'medical' cure for my habit of sucking my fingers. She dipped them in a glass of water filled with pepper powder. Next time my fingers went in my mouth, my lips and tongue caught fire. Or so it seemed. My disgusted face made Lorraine squeal with laughter. To this day I still don't like pepper.

Another time she was playing hairdressers – she was the hairdresser, naturally, and I was the customer. So she fetched Mum's kitchen scissors and happily snip snapped all round my shoulders and then, gaining confidence, chopped my fringe right off.

I wasn't bothered. It was quite interesting watching the dark brown strands cascading all over the kitchen floor. And Lorraine even swept them up afterwards with the carpet sweeper – which was thoughtful of her. But it didn't help. Poor Mum was livid when she got home and saw my butchered locks. I think I had to have a trip to the real hairdresser's after that.

It wasn't just Lorraine of course. I was quite capable of dreaming up my own escapades. I particularly enjoyed taking various jars and packets and bottles out of the cupboard and mixing them all together in Mum's big bowl to make different potions. Some of the creations were reasonably tasty too. Lorraine got to sample quite a few, some of them admittedly disgusting but others quite reasonable. Of course, lost in our own MasterChef games we failed to notice the greasy streaks down the kitchen cupboards or the fact that when Mum next went to use a particular condiment, she'd discover the container practically empty.

Poor Mum, she never knew what she'd find when she got home – and it wasn't much use trying to discipline us either.

She'd send us to our rooms in disgrace when we'd done something particularly naughty but it wasn't much of a punishment. We just carried on playing happily together upstairs. There was only one effective deterrent that worked every time.

'Right!' she'd say. 'Bewitched is on and you're missing it. You're not going to see it!'

That did it. We were heartbroken. Bewitched, starring Elizabeth Montgomery as a suburban housewife who was also secretly a witch, was our favourite TV show. But there were no TVs in bedrooms in those days and certainly no Wifi or laptops. The only TV set was downstairs with Mum and Dad – and we were currently banished. When Mum said 'no' it meant 'NO.'

Missing a single episode was a dreadful blow. We'd be little angels, we promised if only we could watch Bewitched! As if!

Mum's name was Doris and Dad was Joe and apparently both their families originated many generations back, in Poland. Neither Mum nor Dad could speak Polish but they were both fluent in the old fashioned language of Yiddish. Sadly neither Lorraine nor I mastered this art, which seems to be dying out now, but it was very useful at the time. As children we were always amazed when, on holidays abroad, Mum and Dad, despite having no Italian or Spanish, or wherever we happened to be, were soon chatting happily away to other foreign holiday-makers who were Jewish, in this communal language they all seemed to know. They made a lot of new friends in this way.

Although in the years before World War 2 their two families didn't know each other, both ended up settling for a time in the East End, where one grandfather worked as a milliner, and the other a tailor. Then not long before the war, Dad's family moved to South Africa for a while. Mum's stayed in Stepney until their house was flattened by a doodle bug – the first of the war.

Mum, her sister and mother were evacuated to Bedford for the duration but by the early '50s Dad's family had returned from South Africa owing to Grandma Esther's homesickness. They gravitated to Baker Street, while Mum's family resettled in Stamford Hill, London.

Oddly enough, though Mum and Dad were both back in London after the war, they actually met, miles away in Brighton. Then as now, lively Brighton with its iconic pier and pebbly beach, was a cool place for young Londoners to hang out. So one warm summer weekend in 1957 both Mum and Dad happened to set off for a day at the seaside with their respective friends.

At some point Mum and her girlfriends were sitting on the seafront soaking up the sun, when Dad and his group wandered by. Dad was very handsome in those days with his dark hair and bright blue eyes, while Mum was a stunner with the tiniest waist you've ever seen.

They couldn't help but notice each other. And of course Dad with his cheeky personality and gift of the gab didn't take long in striking up a conversation. People always used to say he had such a charming, persuasive way about him he could sell sand to the Arabs. So much so that later, on our holidays, the other holidaymakers would persuade Dad to go with them when they were buying souvenirs because they knew he'd bargain with the shopkeepers and not only get them the best price but also a free gift thrown in as well.

So of course that day on Brighton seafront it wasn't long before Dad had linked himself to Mum's group and the rest is history. They were married within the year.

Though both were brought up in the Jewish faith neither of them was particularly religious. Mum's family had been quite orthodox and as a result she took our heritage and the Jewish traditions very seriously, while Dad, whose family was not strict at all, was happy enough to go along with the various rituals for Mum's sake. The result was we celebrated all the local religious festivals – Jewish and Christian - so Lorraine and I grew up enjoying the best of both worlds.

It was puzzling to me how controversial this Kosher business – required by our religion - seemed to be. When Lorraine and I visited our Grandma Esther on Dad's side of the family for the day, she'd fry up a pack of Walls pork sausages for us. How I loved those pork sausages. They were so delicious, yet we never had them at home. Gradually I began to understand these were forbidden fruit in some way.

Mum was obviously not pleased about Grandma feeding us pork. Yet she never complained. Grandma was doing her a favour after all and we were in Grandma's home so she didn't feel it was her place to speak out.

It was the war years that turned Grandma into a rebel. Apparently she noticed the way any item labelled 'Kosher' was instantly far more expensive than the non-Kosher equivalent and she realised that quite a few unscrupulous shopkeepers were labelling non-Kosher foods as Kosher, simply to charge higher prices.

She came to her own conclusion it was all a 'racket', it was impossible to be sure what you were buying so she might as well ignore the whole thing. It wasn't long before Grandma's relaxed attitude to the food traditions permeated down to Dad and the rest of her family.

Mum, who came from a much more orthodox background, struggled valiantly to do the right thing in the teeth of this indifference. The story was often told of how early in their marriage, before they moved to Edgware, Mum and Dad lived near my Grandma and Grandpa in Shepherd's Bush and on the Eve of the Passover celebration Mum went out to buy their special Passover food.

Passover requires extra sensitively refined Kosher food I learned. To mark it out from the ordinary Kosher food, each item bears the label 'Kosher for Passover'. So that day Mum bought all the usual treats, heaved her loaded bags back to the flat, only to discover she'd forgotten the pickled cucumber – a particular favourite.

So being Mum, she turned right round and went back to the shop.

'I've forgotten the pickled cucumber,' she told the shopkeeper.

'I think it's all gone,' he said. Then he stopped. 'Oh, just a minute. I'll have a look.'

Off he went and came back a minute or two later with a jar of ordinary pickled cucumber. Then he took out his label-maker, painstakingly punched in the words 'Kosher for Passover', peeled off the new label and stuck it carefully on the jar.

'There you are,' he said, 'Kosher for Passover pickled cucumber.'

And despite the fact she'd watched him brazenly create a fake Passover item, Mum actually bought the cucumber!

She was teased about it ever afterwards and of course it proved Grandma Esther's point. Nevertheless, Mum carried on. She kept milk and meat in separate places in the fridge. We never ate milky sauces or cheese with meat. In fact we never ate milk in a meal at all if even one of the courses contained meat. In later years though, she wasn't sure what to do when begged for ice-cream for dessert. Ice cream became a bit of a grey area and Lorraine and I were often allowed a scoop or two as a treat.

Following the traditions wasn't easy for Mum. As a small child I remember Mum having to Kosher her own meat. A meat delivery would arrive not long after Mum got in from work and while simultaneously cooking the family meal, Mum would rush from the stove to the big bowl where she washed the meat, salted it, left it for a while and returned to stir dinner on the stove. Then she was back to the bowl again later to wash the meat for a second time. She'd be so tired she could hardly stand up – because of course she'd already been standing all day in the shop - but she doggedly persevered until the whole batch was purified and deemed

Kosher.

I suppose being so young, the significance of Mum's effort passed me by. It was just what she did. Normal life. It was only a few years later I realised how much these things meant to her.

It was a Saturday morning and while Mum and Dad were at work, one of our cousins came to play. One of our older cousins from Dad's relaxed side of the family! Jilly brought her lunch with her and Lorraine and I were thrilled to see the lunch naughtily consisted of a big tin of frankfurters. Another delicacy we'd never sampled.

We knew quite well these were sausages of some kind and that Mum didn't allow these sausages. But Mum was out. So we heated up the frankfurters, scoffed the lot – blissful they were too – and then cleared away the evidence before Mum came home.

Unfortunately, later that evening Mum went to throw something away and spotted an unfamiliar tin in the bin. Out it came and the guilty frankfurters were discovered in all their shame.

Mum was furious. Almost crosser than I'd ever seen her. Maybe it was because the sacrilege occurred under her roof, maybe it was because her bin was contaminated or maybe it was because we'd disobeyed her deliberately, I don't know, but she was livid. Angrily she demanded to know which plate we'd put the frankfurters on and Lorraine and I nervously fetched it for her.

Mum took the plate, stared at it in disgust, then smashed it to pieces on the floor so it could never be used again.

Lorraine and I exchanged frightened looks. Such extremes! Such drama! We hadn't quite realised until that moment how seriously Mum took these rules and how important they were to her, but we did now.

We looked with new respect at Mum's Passover dinner service in the cupboard after that. I rather liked that dinner service. It was pale pink with scalloped edges and was the prettiest china in the house in my opinion. Yet it only came out once year, at Passover which seemed a shame.

Mum explained how when she was first married, she spotted the dinner service in the market but couldn't afford it. So the stallholder let her buy it, one plate a week until after several months she had the whole set. No wonder she took such care of it. In fact, it's still intact and in the family.

We had our ups and downs like any family of course but we were a tight-knit, secure unit. And Lorraine and I were quite capable of behaving well when it was absolutely necessary.

Mum and Dad worked so hard that by the time I went to school they were in the habit of taking a much needed week's holiday, just the two of them, during the winter term. Lorraine and I were dispatched to a kindly Aunt for the duration. I loved this Auntie, she was like a second Mum to me and we always enjoyed staying with her. Yet by the time Lorraine was 14 and I was 11 we decided Mum and Dad were treating us like babies by sending us away. We were insulted, we protested, that they didn't consider sophisticated sisters like us, old enough to take care of ourselves. We moaned and complained so much about being uprooted from our own beds and farmed out to relatives that in the end our parents agreed to let us stay home alone.

Mum cooked up a week's worth of individual dinners, clearly labelled them and put them in the freezer so all we needed to do was defrost them and warm them through when we got home from school. No doubt she primed Auntie to be on stand-by in case of emergencies and she left us a long list of instructions, plus copious phone numbers.

I expect she was worried sick but they did go, Lorraine and I were left to fend for ourselves and we were absolutely fine and loved the freedom.

Looking back now though, I'm pretty amazed. Times have changed so much I'm sure Mum and Dad would be highly criticised today.

'You'd be charged with neglect these days!' we used to tease Mum. But in truth we came to no harm and at 14 Lorraine really was perfectly capable of looking after herself and of me.

All in all I was very happy at home but the same couldn't be said of school. I just didn't take to school. Somehow I didn't seem to fit in. I was very quiet and shy. The other children made me tongue-tied and nervous. I didn't understand it at the time but I was constantly picking up on their varying, wildly changing emotions and it made me feel confused and mentally battered. So much so that I refused to go on school holiday trips – which isolated me even more.

I didn't specially enjoy lessons either, though I was surprised to find I seemed to have an aptitude for maths. All went well for a while, but then praise from the maths teacher and my high scores in a maths test were noticed by some of the other girls and they began picking on me. I gave up after that. I stopped trying. It just wasn't worth being bullied over.

I clearly wasn't destined for a life in academia but to be honest, I couldn't care less. I wasn't even particularly ambitious. It was as if I sensed, deep down there was a different path for me.

FOUR:

'Where are you in the room, Spirit?' asked Jilly.

It was Christmas Eve and as usual I was desperately trying to stay awake to catch a glimpse of Santa Claus. As I said earlier, strictly speaking we were Jewish, but we happily adopted the Christian festivals as well as the Jewish celebrations and like most children in our neighbourhood, we especially loved Christmas.

But lately there'd been disturbing rumours going round school. Some of the girls said perhaps Santa wasn't real. Perhaps it was really your Dad, who crept in while you were fast asleep and left all those presents! I didn't believe that for a second of course but I was determined to stay up and see Santa for myself, just in case. Actually I tried to see Santa every year but somehow, no matter how hard I tried, I never managed it.

Well this Christmas Eve it was going to be different. I propped my eyelids open and stared out into the blackness for hours on end. Long after Lorraine, who shared the room, had drifted off. I stared into the dark till my eyes were sore. Yet somehow, despite my determination, my treacherous eyelashes fluttered closed and I dozed.

I woke suddenly, goodness knows how long afterwards, really annoyed with myself. It was still dark and I could still hear Lorraine's rhythmic breathing in the next bed so hopefully I hadn't missed anything.

But there was a faint light coming from the foot of my bed. I raised myself on my pillow to see better and realised there was someone sitting there, just below my feet. Disappointingly it wasn't Santa, it was an elderly woman.

She had dark auburn hair, glasses, a brown dress and she was knitting. Her busy needles were clacking back and forth and she kept tugging more yarn from a large ball of wool near my feet. As I stared, she seemed to sense I was awake. She glanced up at me, over the top of her glasses and smiled sweetly.

'It's alright,' she said, expertly hooking yarn round the top of one needle, 'You can go back to sleep. Your toys will be here soon.'

And even more annoyingly, I did.

The next thing I knew it was just about dawn. The woman had gone but there was an exciting pile of brightly wrapped parcels on the floor near where she'd been sitting.

'Come on Lorraine!' I shouted leaping out of bed, the strange woman forgotten, 'Wake up! He's been!'

The only disappointing part of the morning was that once again Santa had failed to bring Lorraine and I the real, live puppy we'd asked for. He never did. In later years we begged Dad to buy us a dog but *he* never did either.

Poor Mum and Dad. We used to drive them mad about having a dog. They always refused on the grounds they were both out at work all day and it wasn't right to leave a dog alone for hours on end, but being young and immature, Lorraine and I couldn't understand this reasoning.

We pestered so much that one Christmas both Lorraine and I opened our parcels to find we'd each received a battery operated pup.

Dad thought these toys were amusing substitutes for the real thing. They strutted and flipped and turned somersaults and he and Mum found them hilarious. The pair of them laughed aloud at the dog's jerky, mechanical antics. But stony-faced, Lorraine and I refused to see the funny side. In fact I think we privately agreed not to speak to Mum and Dad for weeks.

At night the knitting lady continued to visit from time to time. Who she was I didn't know – I still don't - but I wasn't scared. She was a gentle, reassuring presence. I'd lay watching her hypnotic needles working away, the wool swaying from side to side, until my eyelids grew heavy and I fell asleep.

I was still nervous of the globes of light. Sometimes so many filled the room it was like an indoor snowstorm. I was fascinated more than anything. Sometimes I beckoned them closer so I could see them properly. They'd grow brighter and brighter and larger and larger as they approached my pillow, but when they were only inches from my nose I'd get scared and pull the covers over my head. Not before I'd glimpsed what looked like faces inside though.

They were baffling but seemed like natural phenomena somehow. A normal part of the night – even though other people never mentioned them. Certainly Lorraine was always asleep when they materialised. These random appearances grew so familiar, so ordinary to me, I no longer bothered talking about them. Lorraine never referred to them so I was pretty sure she hadn't seen them and Mum and Dad made it perfectly clear they thought I was dreaming or making up stories, so I quickly concluded there was no point in saying anything.

Strangely enough, though Mum gave the impression such fanciful notions were nonsense, or if not nonsense, probably against our religion and best not delved into, Dad was much more open to psychic ideas.

I didn't realise it till years later but apparently Dad came from a long line of healers and he was instinctively drawn to spiritual matters. He used to go to watch a famous medium and healer of the day called Joe Benjamin. In fact at one demonstration, Joe Benjamin apparently picked Dad out of the large audience and told him he was a natural healer too. He was gifted with healing hands said Joe.

Sadly Dad never attempted to explore any skill he might have in this direction – he was far too busy with the shop - but he had a lot of time for spiritual healing. Years before, he'd been involved in an accident that left him with a limp and recurring back problems. He had an operation but it didn't seem to improve matters so these days and when the discomfort got bad, he'd fallen into the habit of visiting a healing sanctuary not far from us in north London.

I was fascinated to know what went on there so when I too began to have problems with my lower back – I think it was a slipped disc - Mum reluctantly agreed that he could take me along on his next visit. After all, even if it didn't do any good it wouldn't do any harm. I was thrilled.

So after school one evening, Dad picked me up and drove us the few miles through the suburban streets. Eventually he pulled up in a quiet, tree lined road a few miles from our home and I peered out eagerly at a beautiful old Victorian house set back from the pavement.

Even from the car I could feel the wonderful, vibrant energy that seemed to flow out from the plot in great, exuberant waves. The whole building appeared to be floating in vivid green. Ivy scrambled up the walls. Shrubs and vigorous trees spread across the garden, lush flowers crowded round their feet and little birds flitted through the bushes. Abundant life seemed to be bursting out everywhere.

It was like stepping into another world. Dad led me along a winding path through the foliage up to the front door, exotic with an antique stained glass panel, and then we were being ushered inside. I stared around in amazement. Anywhere less like our modern orange and tan semi in Edgware was hard to imagine. The house was dimly lit, there were patterned Victorian tiles on the floor, big old lanterns hanging from the ceiling and great leafy plants in huge ceramic pots everywhere you looked. Soft music was playing in the background and a feeling of peace and serenity seemed settled over the whole place like a goose-down duvet.

Just then an elderly couple, Bill and Evelyn, Dad called them, moved quietly out of the shadows to say hello. They were wearing white coats like doctors and their faces seemed to me to shine with compassion. They led us through to their healing room where we were directed to make ourselves comfortable on the special beds. Then aided by an assistant, they worked in silence, placing their hands gently on our feet, our heads and so on while we lay back and relaxed. I could hardly feel their touch but I was aware of all tension gradually sliding away, my mind began to drift and drift until I felt as if I was floating.

I have no idea how long the healing lasted. I lost all track of time, floating there perfectly happy and content. But after a while, Bill and Evelyn stepped back and I realised they'd finished. An assistant helped me to my feet and Dad and I were led to another room furnished with big comfy sofas and armchairs.

'Now just have a rest there for a while dear,' said Evelyn pointing me towards an inviting armchair, 'Give the healing time to manifest.' and the next thing I knew I was lazing in deep, velvety cushions half asleep.

By the time we returned to the car, half an hour later I was on cloud 9 and my back felt fine. 'When can we go again Dad?' I asked. I loved it.

Encouraged by my interest, Dad lent me a book he'd bought recently which he thought explained psychic matters in a way I'd understand. It was called Voices in My Ear by a medium named Doris Stokes. It was amazing. I was enthralled. I'd never read a book by a medium before and I couldn't put it down. Little did I know that Doris would have special significance for me in years to come!

Back home, where practical matters were uppermost, I was

trying to get to grips with the traditions of Judaism to please Mum. We weren't regulars at the synagogue due to Mum and Dad's work but Mum tried to observe the high holy days and holidays as best she could.

There was one celebration called Simchat Torah in which we children marched around in a procession waving a flag which had an eating apple stuck on the top. I didn't quite understand what it was all about but somehow, by the end of the parade there was a core on the top of my flag instead of a rosy apple!

Then there was the holy day of Yom Kippur, the most important day of the Jewish calendar when you were supposed to repent your sins and fast for 25 hours. 'God's watching you. He knows everything you do.' we were told sternly. But I was puzzled. If he already knew what we'd been up to, why did he want us to tell him about it now?

It was a kind of day of mourning. Dad wasn't even allowed to smoke which was very difficult for him. We all tried to keep out of his way that day as he'd be in such a bad mood.

Friday evenings were easier to understand. Friday evenings were the Sabbath and we didn't go out. Even as teenagers Lorraine and I were expected to stay home. Mum was a great cook and she always made us a lovely dinner – a tasty roast, with chicken soup or chopped liver to start and apple pie to finish. Then we spent a cosy evening round the TV. No homework or work of any kind was allowed on a Friday night – which was fine by me!

Yet despite mum's best efforts, the spirit world kept crossing my path. We often went to visit relatives in Essex – from Dad's side of the family and Lorraine and I always ended up hanging out with our cousin Jilly. Mum probably thought the three of us were busy enjoying some harmless, childish fun, but then she had no idea what sort of games we played!

We'd tear up to Jilly's bedroom – the little box-room at the front of the house – shut the door tight, sprawl across Jilly's bed and wait for Jilly to get out her Ouija Board. Ouija Boards were quite fashionable back then and were regarded as simple board games, no more serious than Cluedo or Monopoly or Snakes and Ladders. Quite a few children had them. I know now they're dangerous things and would certainly not advise playing with them but back then I assumed this was a game like any other.

Lorraine and Jilly showed me a small, tear-drop shaped piece of plastic which was called a 'planchette'. All you had to do was put your finger on the planchette and lightly steer it round and round the board which was printed with the letters of the alphabet. Then you asked a question and the 'planchette' would obligingly drag your finger towards letter after letter until it had miraculously spelled out an answer. The correct answer, hopefully.

'From the spirits!' giggled Jilly in a spooky voice.

To be honest I was a bit nervous. I wasn't sure I liked the sound of this game, but anxious not to look like a baby in front of the big girls, I pretended to be cool with the idea.

Jilly demonstrated pushing the planchette around to show how it was done. After a bit she said it was moving under its own steam and pulling her hand towards various letters. She swore she wasn't cheating. 'Ok. So now you have to ask the spirit where it is in the room,' she explained. 'Where are you in the room, Spirit?' she called.

In spite of myself I stared in fascination as the little plastic tear drop began to move, all on its own Jilly insisted, across the board – as if in answer. It came to rest pointing towards the B…it paused for a moment, then off it went again…'O'… it said. Then it set off towards 'T', then another 'T' Soon it became clear it had spelled the word BOTTOM – which might have been funny for nine year old me, had it stopped there. But it didn't. 'O…F' it continued. and then after a longer pause:

B.E.V.E.R.L.E.Y'S… F.E.E.T.

Bottom of Beverley's feet! Horrified, I yanked my feet off the floor and pulled them onto the bed. I couldn't see anything down there but I was totally freaked out.

'I don't like this! I don't want to play anymore,' I cried, 'I'm going back to Mum.' And with that I jumped up and ran downstairs.

For a while after that I refused to join in with the Ouija Board games but Jilly and Lorraine carried on, and bit by bit my curiosity got the better of my nerves. In the end I was lured back to our mini séances.

The strange thing was we usually got messages that made sense and were correct. Frequently, when we asked who we were talking to, the communicators would spell out their names and they were names we recognised. Mostly long departed aunts and uncles from our family. Occasionally they were people we'd never heard of but later when we asked our parents, we invariably discovered these unknowns were actually real, distant relatives.

This was intriguing but I was still uneasy. Particularly as when we asked the spirits where they were in the room, they would usually mention my name. I didn't like that at all.

It never occurred to me to connect these peculiar, invisible messengers with the shining globes I saw at night, or the old lady who liked to knit at the end of my bed. It would be a long time before all the pieces of the jigsaw would fall into place.

FIVE:

'We can't help...
this is your Dad's time...'

I stared at my reflection in the mirror as I freshened up my lipstick. Nope, still couldn't see it myself but these days, people often called me 'Princess Di' because they reckoned I looked just like her.

It was March 1983 and our new Princess of Wales was the biggest star of the era. The celebrity who put all other celebrities in the shade. Every single week, at least one magazine on every news-stand would feature Princess Diana on the cover – for the very good reason, the editors explained, that any issue featuring HRH immediately sold out.

We couldn't get enough of her back then. Not just me. A huge section of the public followed the princess's every move and every outfit. We admired her clothes, her style and her cheeky sense of humour, combined with that shy smile. So of course, I was highly flattered when people saw a resemblance.

I was nowhere near as tall as the lovely Di of course but I'd brightened my mousey brown locks to blonde, had my cut hair in a similar flicky style and often wore a high-necked frilly white blouse like she did, so maybe that was it.

Anyway, this particular evening I was out with my friend Lorri. We'd recently been on a wonderful, girlie holiday to Corfu and we'd met up tonight to have a laugh over our photos, reminisce about our hilarious Greek adventures and maybe plan our next expedition.

I was wearing my highly fashionable one-piece jump-suit, known in those days as a boiler-suit, for the occasion. I loved that outfit. Jumpsuits were so comfortable to wear once you got them on, though rather complicated when you needed the Ladies'. But hey, that's fashion! Anyway, jumpsuit, lipstick and flicky hair fully restored in the loo, I headed back out to Lorri and our table.

We were actually on our second location of the evening. After a meal in a nearby restaurant we hadn't nearly exhausted our conversation so we moved on down the road to a coffee bar that stayed open late.

And soon, not long after I resumed my seat, a guy who'd been sitting nearby and making cheeky comments in our direction, came over to join us. Then he was joined by his friend Simon. We didn't think anything of it but there was a definite spark between Simon and me. After that, we kept meeting up. We discovered we had other friends in common and soon we were hanging out in a big group.

Strange isn't it, how often you just know someone's going to be special? The upshot was Simon and I started seeing each other. By coincidence my sister Lorraine was getting married the following month and even though it was just a few weeks after our first meeting, I invited Simon to the wedding.

Miraculously he melted into my family almost like one of our relatives. I was glad to see that Mum and Dad took to him at once. So much so Mum even forgave him for the dining-room chair incident. As for Simon's family they welcomed me into the huge Mann clan.

Simon was a student at the time, aiming at becoming a chartered surveyor, while I was still unsure what I wanted to do. I'd left school, grateful to get out, took a bilingual secretarial course – French being the second language I chose - then drifted through a number of jobs. Some of them were quite glamorous. Most exciting was a stint at Rank Films Publicity Department where I was able to attend all the film premieres and meet some of the stars. Yet it was never long before I got bored and moved on for a change of scene.

At one point I found myself working for a firm of solicitors. My boss specialised in conveyancing and I worked so closely with him and got to learn so much about the ins and outs of the legal work I began to get a real feel for it. So much so I reckoned I could do it myself. In the end I asked my boss and the partners of the firm if they would let me take a part-time legal course to become qualified myself. To my delight, they agreed and soon Simon and I were spending our evenings studying together – him with his array of technical books and me with my legal tomes.

Amazingly we both passed our exams. Simon became a chartered surveyor and I became a legal executive. I spent many fulfilling months helping council house tenants buy their council homes under a new right to buy scheme the government had launched. It was hard work but so rewarding when you saw how pleased they were to own their property – something many of them thought they'd never be able to do.

By this time, the strange lights and spirit visitors I used to see in my room at night had almost faded away. My life was so busy and so full of excitement I hardly gave that puzzling phenomena a thought.

Besides, Simon and I were getting married in September 1987. There was a wedding to arrange and a first home to buy. The old night terrors were a distant memory.

Mum was in her element of course, fussing over the wedding details. We toured just about every wedding shop in London trying on bridal gowns. Yet somehow I couldn't find anything quite right. Princess Diana had set a new fashion in wedding dresses a few years before with her memorable Cinderella style crinoline, so now of course most brides glided down the aisle in something similar. But though people still thought we looked alike, the Diana voluminous design swamped my small frame. It just wasn't me at all. I thought I'd look like one of those novelty doll toilet-roll holders.

Then when I'd almost given up hope, I found the perfect gown – quite unlike the others. It was a lovely, white satin dress, covered in tiny seed pearls. It fitted sleekly over the waist and hips, then flared out mermaid style in wafts of white tulle to my feet. It could have been made specially for me. Mum was almost in tears when I emerged from the changing room.

Our wedding day, September 6th dawned disappointingly overcast, but somehow the clouds couldn't spoil the lovely day. Dad and I were whisked to the Edgware Synagogue in a white Rolls Royce for the traditional ceremony. Then we all moved on to the reception at the nearby Hilton Hotel where we enjoyed a delicious five course dinner. Later a ten-piece band arrived and we danced the night away.

The next day, after a big family lunch Simon and I – the brand new Mr & Mrs - flew off to Kenya for our honeymoon. It was certainly a memorable trip. So memorable we almost didn't survive it!

We were combining a beach holiday in Mombasa with a few days in the bush – where we were to be taken on a mini safari. So exciting! After a day or two relaxing at our ocean view hotel, we eagerly boarded a small plane to fly out to the wilderness. Then from the plane we were loaded into Land Rovers to drive off in search of Big Game. There were zebra, elephants and lions, we were assured. We might even spy the rare and endangered white rhino.

I was thrilled. Everything was quite magical as we bumped along the dusty dirt track through the acacia trees. We caught sight of zebra and wildebeeste and lions and it was all like a David Attenborough documentary come to life - until suddenly, we stumbled across a huge bull elephant – in a very bad mood.

I don't know what had upset him, maybe he didn't like our vehicles passing through but whatever the cause, he threw a massive temper tantrum. For a moment he just stood there glaring at us with his huge ears flapping, then he made a very threatening, ear-splitting cry and started to charge towards us. I hadn't realised until that moment just how enormous a full grown bull elephant can be.

Our driver immediately put the Land Rover into reverse and we shot back, only to get stuck in a patch of mud. The wheels were spinning, the elephant racing closer, trunk waving angrily and I clutched Simon's hand in terror. At the very last second our frantic driver managed to get the wheels to grip, the Land Rover spun round and we tore away in a cloud of dust and mud.

Whew! That was close! We laughed about it afterwards as, safari over, we headed for our luxury camp near a picturesque water hole. We were rather dusty and mud spattered now and still a bit shaky.

'Well I never expected the wild life to be quite so wild!' I said to Simon as we climbed out of the Land Rover, 'I'll be glad to get in for a shower! Still, at least we're safe!'

It hadn't struck me till that moment, that when you're actually there, rather than watching it all on TV, your safety can't be guaranteed 100%.

And it wasn't just the wild animals that could be dangerous. A couple of days later we climbed back into the tiny plane for the return trip to Mombasa. Hardly had we taken off than clouds appeared from nowhere and our fragile little aircraft hit massive turbulence over Mount Kilimanjaro.

We bounced about all over the sky and at times we dropped so fast I was sure we were going to crash. I clung to Simon in terror once more. 'If we ever get out of this alive I'll never complain about anything ever again,' I shouted into his ear, trying not to scream as the acacia treetops rushed up towards us alarmingly, 'This could be one of the shortest marriages in history!'

Fortunately, though I don't know how he did it, the pilot managed to keep control of the plane as it bucked about like a wild pony but eventually, we landed, heavily but in one piece in Mombasa. We stumbled out onto the simple airstrip, shell shocked. I'm sure more than one of our party was tempted to kiss the ground like the Pope does when he steps off a plane. We all needed a very stiff drink after that!

I'm glad to say the last few days of our honeymoon were more restful and we had a wonderful time. Side by side on the reassuringly large and comfortable jet, UK bound, Simon and I began to see the funny side of our adventure. Well we'd never forget our honeymoon, that's for sure, we laughed. And if we'd made it through such an experience unscathed, surely we could survive anything?

Back in Britain, we settled into our new home in North West London. We'd bought a first floor maisonette overlooking a spacious, green common – a peaceful spot, yet right at the end of the underground line, convenient for getting into the city and convenient for visiting my parents in Edgware.

Simon and I were very happy there. The place had its little quirks of course. There was something odd about the narrow doors on the built-in wardrobes for instance. We weren't bothered, but knowing the previous owner had been a funeral director, we used to joke the doors must have been made out of coffin lids! Somehow they only added to our home's eccentric charm.

We'd always wanted a family but we were still young, so we spent the first few years of our marriage just enjoying being a couple. A year or two after our wedding my dad was taken very ill with cancer. It was a dreadful time. He nearly died. Fortunately, after a major operation during which he had to be put on a ventilator he recovered and came home. We breathed a sigh of relief.

The good news continued. Early in 1990 I discovered I was pregnant. We were thrilled. Simon was delighted to think he was about to become a father, and Mum and Dad were overjoyed that their first grandchild was on its way.

Mum and I spent many happy hours discussing cribs, nursery colours, whether I was resting enough and what I was eating. And I reluctantly put away my highest, prettiest heels as my baby bump grew. Couldn't risk toppling over now!

Everything was going well. My consultant was pleased with my progress. There was no reason to suspect there would be any problems, until just before Christmas, when I was 8 months pregnant there came a devastating blow.

We'd been so caught up in baby developments we'd scarcely noticed that Dad wasn't looking too well these days. It turned out he hadn't been feeling too good either. He didn't want to worry us so he didn't say much about it but after a while, he went to the doctor. The doctor promptly sent him to hospital for more tests.

Naturally we were concerned, but not too concerned. After all Dad was only 66 and he'd come through his previous illness very well. He was tough and in good spirits and so looking forward to the new baby.

A few days later his results were due. 'I'll call the consultant for you if you like,' I told mum who was nervous she might not understand the medical terms, or ask the right questions.

It took me a while to get through but when the great man finally came to the phone he was blunt and to the point.

'You know your father's not got long to live,' he said brusquely.

I was so shocked the phone almost slipped out of my hand. 'What?' I said, 'What d'you mean?'

'I'm afraid the cancer's come back and it's inoperable now. It's gone to the liver.'

'But surely… there's some medication… radiotherapy… something…' I managed to croak out.

'I'm sorry. He's already had all the treatment possible. There's nothing more we can do for him.'

I couldn't believe it. This bombshell was so out of the blue. And how could it happen just a few short weeks before he became a grandpa? I could hardly speak but somehow I forced the words out. 'But his first grandchild is due next month. He's so looking forward to it.'

The consultant didn't know what to say to that…

I took a deep breath to steady my voice. I had to be practical. 'How long has he got?'

'Nine days - if he's lucky,' said the consultant.

I was horrified. Nine days! So short a time. How could the universe be so cruel as to cheat him out of becoming a grandfather? And so very, very close, to that great event too. The baby was due towards the end of January.

When I put the phone down I was distraught. Devastated for me, devastated for Dad and devastated for mum. Oh no, Mum! Somehow I was going to have to break the news to her, and to Lorraine.

So that's how what should have been one of the happiest times of my life turned into one of the saddest.

We decided not to tell Dad the bad news. We were looking after him at home and we all struggled to put on brave faces in front of him.

'I know I'm going to die,' he kept saying but we did our best to jolly him out of depressed moods. We tried to give him the will to carry on by talking about the future and how lovely it would be to have a baby in the family again.

But the baby! My pregnancy was suffering under the terrible strain. I couldn't eat, I couldn't sleep, my stomach felt as if it was churning all the time and when no one was around I kept bursting into tears. When I went for my next check-up the consultant was concerned.

'You're losing weight,' he said, 'And you should be putting it on.'

It was quite obvious something was wrong, so I explained the sad situation at home. Fortunately, the consultant was understanding. He didn't make me feeling guilty, but: 'For the baby's sake though. You must try to look after yourself. You must eat.'

I nodded, clutching a tissue to wipe my eyes again.

'Well I'd like to see you back here next week I think,' he said, 'and we'll see how you're getting on.'

I drove straight back to Mum and Dad's feeling a failure. I was doing my best, I really was but it was all so difficult, I was on an emotional roller-coaster. Indoors I considered heading for the kitchen to make a snack to please the consultant but suddenly I was too exhausted, physically and mentally for food.

'I think I'll go up and have a rest on my old bed,' I told mum.

Up in the bedroom I kicked off my shoes, laid down on top of the duvet and tried to sleep. It was no use of course. The minute I closed my eyes I could see Dad's gaunt face in my mind and the same old anxious thoughts started circling round and round.

Suddenly I had an idea. The healing sanctuary from long ago! Surely they could help? I sat bolt upright again. There was a phone on the bedside table so quickly, I dialled the familiar old number.

To my relief the phone was answered almost immediately and amazingly it was Evelyn herself who'd picked up.

'Evelyn I don't know if you remember me,' I said eagerly. 'I used to come with my Dad, Joe. He was one of your regulars.'

'Of course. I remember you both,' said Evelyn kindly.

'Well the thing is,' I went on, 'Dad's very ill with cancer. I was wondering if you could do anything…send him absent healing or something…help him get better.'

The weird thing was, even though we hadn't seen her for years it was almost as if she was expecting me to call. It was like she already knew about Dad's condition.

There was a long silence. Then:

'I'm awfully sorry dear,' she said gently, 'There's nothing more we can do. I'm afraid this is your Dad's time.'

I was horrified. 'How do you know that?' I cried, 'How can you know that?'

'I'm so sorry dear,' said Evelyn, 'We can't do what you want. It's his time. We will pray for you both.'

I put the phone down, hardly noticing the tears splashing over the receiver. How could she say that? How could she know? Surely there must be something that could be done.

'Why don't you help him?' I shouted out loud to the ceiling, in frustration, anger and grief. I'm not sure who I thought I was talking to. I certainly wasn't expecting an answer. 'He needs your help! Please help!'

Suddenly it was as if someone had switched on a light. The brightest radiance I'd ever seen flooded into the bedroom and a great golden ball of light appeared from nowhere and was descending slowly towards me. I could feel an amazing warmth on my skin and my eyes were dazzled. The huge globe blazed brighter and brighter until the whole room was glowing like the Sun – it was like being inside the Sun. I was surrounded, enveloped, completely bathed in brilliance. At the same time the most wonderful feeling of calm and happiness and peace swept through me. It was as if the light itself was made of pure tranquillity and joy.

I sat there for a moment soaking up the miraculous blaze, too stunned to think straight. Then my brain whirred back into life. Somehow I understood this was an answer. My prayer had been heard. But they'd got the wrong end of the stick.

'Not me!' I cried to the light! 'Go to my dad! Take it to him. He needs your help.'

There was a brief pause, then instantly the light was gone and the room went dark.

Did it move on to my father? Who can tell? He didn't mention any strange experience. Yet the odd thing was, he hung on. Nine days came and went and he was still here. I felt better too. The serenity of the light seemed to linger. I was still anxious and sad, yet somehow, deep down there was an inner calmness that hadn't been there before.

Eating was still a problem though. I did try to swallow a reasonable amount of food but I simply wasn't hungry and every mouthful seemed to stick in my throat. When I went back to the consultant he was not satisfied. My weight had not picked up, in fact it was still going down.

'This won't do,' he said. My mental state, it seemed, was not good for the baby. For all I knew, my anguish might actually be harming it. But what could I do? The situation was only going to get worse with every passing day. Dad was on borrowed time as it was.

We were into the New Year now – only weeks from the due date.

The consultant was still unhappy about my condition. It was obviously not going to improve so he suggested I had a Caesarean.

'But what about Simon?' I said, 'He's so looking forward to being at the birth. I don't want to cheat him of an irreplaceable experience.'

The consultant raised an eyebrow, 'Well I suppose you could have an elective Caesarean so you'd be awake and your husband would be able to be present – in a gown and wellington boots.'

It seemed like the best solution. Suddenly everything was happening in a hurry. A bed was found, arrangements were made but we decided not to mention anything to Dad in case he worried. We were going to let him think the baby had simply come early. In the meantime, Dad surprised us by asking to see a medium. He'd been in the habit of visiting mediums now and then and fortunately Barbara Evans, one of his favourites was happy to call in and do her best for him.

What happened was just between the two of them but Dad told me afterwards Barbara said January 12th was going to be an important date. Also that the baby was going to be a boy.

I couldn't believe it because unknown to Dad, January 12th was the date the consultant had arranged for me to go in to have my baby.

My bag was packed and the next thing I knew I was being whisked into hospital. Finally, on January 12th Simon and I welcomed our first child into the world. A little boy – just as the medium had predicted.

'I can't understand it,' the gynaecologist said after congratulating us. 'Our radiologist is the best in the field. He's almost never wrong. He was certain it was a girl…'

Simon and I didn't mind either way. We were just delighted to have a happy, healthy baby. This tiny boy was perfect.

We called him James and of course Mum and Dad were completely besotted with him. Dad was very weak and using a wheelchair by now but he insisted mum push him through the cold streets to buy gifts.

Not long afterwards they sailed into the ward, blue and silver balloons streaming out behind the wheelchair and Dad half hidden by an enormous bunch of flowers and a turquoise teddy bear.

He was very frail by now which broke my heart, but the joy on his face as he beamed at his grandson was absolutely priceless. Mum put the baby into his arms and he sat there staring down at the new-born boy, tears in his eyes.

I realised this was the best gift I could possibly give him. Much later it struck me I was actually witnessing the loving answer to my desperate prayer. The light had granted a wish after all. Dad could not be restored to health as I wanted. But he'd been given a few precious extra days so he could hold his beloved grandson in his arms. It was *his* dying wish that had been granted, not mine. But then hadn't I sent the light to him?

Back then when you had a Caesarean you were usually in hospital for a week so I had to spend the next few days learning to care for my baby on the ward. Naturally I was sore from the operation and a bit overwhelmed as most first time mums are, but I was surrounded by cards and flowers, and excited friends dropped in every day.

James was an adorable baby. He had fair hair, big blue eyes and that first week he never seemed to cry.

Even the nurses loved him. 'He looks like a little angel,' they said.

'He is,' I agreed. 'God's sent me an angel to cheer me up.'

Dad managed a couple more trips to visit James. He looked even frailer if anything, but he hugged his beloved grandson, all smart and sweet smelling in a new baby-grow, as if he'd never put him down. After being a dad to two daughters, having a little boy in the family must have been even more special. When it was time to go, he dropped a lingering kiss onto James' forehead and gave me a huge, grateful smile and then Mum was wheeling him away down the corridor.

A couple of days later Lorraine popped in again. She'd been back and forth a few times, so thrilled to be an auntie, but today she had bad news.

'Dad's fading fast,' she said. 'He's not getting out of bed now. The doctor said it might only be hours…'

That did it. 'I've got to go,' I told the nurse. 'I'm going home.'

'You can't,' she said, 'You've not been discharged yet. The

doctor…'

'I don't care about the doctor,' I interrupted, 'My father's dying. I'm discharging myself.'

I phoned Simon and between sobs told him he had to come and get me. The medical staff weren't pleased. They didn't feel I was ready to leave yet but I wouldn't hear of staying a moment longer.

Not long after my call, Simon arrived. Despite disapproving stares all round, we wrapped James in a tiny snowsuit and strapped him into his baby carry-seat. I scooped up armfuls of flowers, cards, china knick-knacks and balloons, hastily thanked all the nurses then we dashed out to the car. I tossed all the pretty gifts into the boot without a second glance and we raced off to Edgware.

I was so confused. Leaving hospital to take our first baby home should have been such a happy, euphoric occasion. Instead all I could feel was sadness and stress. It was a race again time.

That day was the last time I saw Dad alive. He was barely conscious by the time we arrived. After sitting at his bedside, holding his hand with James in my arms, for hours. Finally, I was persuaded to go home to rest and Simon's mum came over to look after the baby in case I got the dreaded phone call in the night.

It came at 5 o clock the next morning – 19 January 1991. My sister phoned with the bad news that Dad was passing away. We raced over as fast as we could, but when we got there the nurse met us at the door.

'Sorry you're too late. He's gone.'

But I could feel him close. I rushed up the stairs. There was Dad lying motionless in bed. I was sure I could hear him breathing.

'No, he's gone,' the nurse insisted.

Yet I could feel Dad's presence. If I reached out I could almost touch it, I was sure. It was almost as if he'd waited for me to arrive. It was exactly one week since James was born.

Later, when we came downstairs from saying goodbye and telling him how much we loved him, I walked into the lounge and switched on the lights. As I watched, the lamp that hung over Dad's special armchair flickered and then suddenly pinged out. The bulb had blown.

Lorraine and I looked at each other. Dad was gone.

Mum and Dad get engaged!

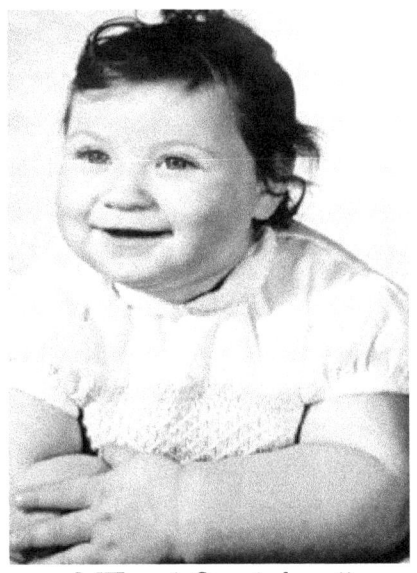

ME - A Star is born!!

The donkey seems just as scared as me on one of our first holidays!

A family event! Don't we scrub up well!

Rocking my '80s boiler suit - against the famous patterned wallpaper!

Getting ready for a night out Diana style!

A legend in action - Dad's shop Brixton market

Grandma Esther and Grandpa Len at their diamond wedding

Papa Maurie and Grandma Sarah (Mum's parents in the '60s)

Me with Mum and Dad on the big day

Dad on the infamous phone!

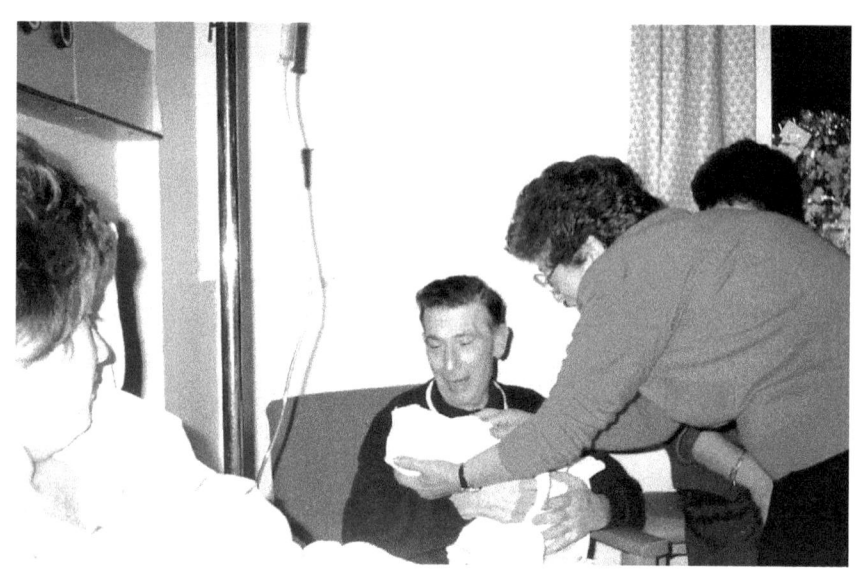

Dad gets to hold baby James - my greatest gift to him

78

Rachel arrives!

My pride and joy - James and Rachel

SIX:

'You should be doing this,' said the Medium...

The medium looked at me a little oddly, though I couldn't quite work out what her expression meant.

Ever since Dad had passed away I'd been trying to get a message from him. Which is how I'd ended up in this psychic lady's eccentrically cluttered home in Hertfordshire.

It might have been small but there was a mysterious air about the unassuming little house in the perfectly ordinary suburban street. Everywhere I looked I saw strange, shadowy corners and Mum would have been amazed at the higgledy-piggledy arrangement of odds and ends that covered every surface. This was clearly an owner who liked to have her treasures close at hand where she could see them.
It was quirky, but in a friendly way, not at all spooky.

'Your dad's very proud of you,' the medium went on, settling down more comfortably in her chair 'And he's talking about James.'

'His grandson,' I said.

'And he's talking about your daughter...'

'He knows about Rachel!' I said in delight. Rachel was our second child – the grand-daughter he'd never seen. I'd been so sad Dad passed away before he could meet her, before he even knew we were having another baby.

'Yes of course he knows,' said the medium. 'They keep an eye on you from the other side, so of course he's seen Rachel.' Then she stopped and gave me that look again. 'You know, you should be doing this.'

I stared at her. 'Sorry? Doing what? What d'you mean?'

'Doing what I'm doing. You can do this,' she insisted.

'Being a medium – like you!?' I had to stop myself from laughing. Surely she wasn't serious. 'Of course I couldn't! I wouldn't know where to start.'

'Yes you can,' she went on, 'You've got the gift.'

I shook my head incredulously. It was the craziest thing I'd ever heard. As if I could talk to dead people!

'Tell me something about myself,' she said, 'Go on. Tell me anything at all that comes to you.'

This was bonkers. I didn't even know her or anything about her. What did she expect me to say? Yet she was staring at me expectantly so I tried to think of something – no matter how ridiculous. Almost immediately a kind of mental picture floated into my mind. I saw a woman struggling with a pram. She had two children, a girl and a boy.

I began describing what I was seeing, out loud.

'The boy's older than the girl,' I went on, 'They've both got fair hair and the little boy's wearing a blue checked jacket. The woman's really struggling. She's having a tough time.

She's finding it very difficult to manage the two children on her own.'

I stopped. The medium was nodding in a: 'told you so' kind of way. 'You've just described my best friend and her children,' she said, 'And you're quite right. She is having a tough time.'

I was shocked. I had no sense of seeing anything significant. It all seemed quite random. It was almost like a daydream. Almost like I was making up a story. I couldn't believe I was talking about real people the medium knew. How could that have happened?

'There you are,' the medium went on, 'You can do it. You should join a developing circle. That way you'll learn to how to use your gift.' She stopped as if some unseen person had just interrupted her and then nodded in their direction. 'Now they're telling me you're going to write three books.'

She really has gone crazy now I thought. Maths had been my thing at school, not essay writing. These days I hardly got time to read a book let alone write one.

Nevertheless, it was an interesting reading on so many levels. Losing Dad had really fired my interest in psychic phenomena. He'd always been open to visiting mediums in the hope of making contact with his departed relatives – and now here I was following in his footsteps, visiting mediums in the hope of making contact with him.

Of course life had gone on after his passing, as it always does, even when you're devastated, but it hadn't been exactly tranquil. We seemed to face one challenge after another.

First, just a few days after Dad died, we followed the tradition in our religion to sit shiva – a period of mourning in which the bereaved sit at home and receive condolences and comfort from visiting family and friends. It usually lasts for a week. Of course it was particularly difficult right now, what with me being such a new mum and recovering from the caesarean operation. We had to get a nurse to look after baby James, still only a week old, and also to check me out. I could barely walk and was still sore from the op.

Nevertheless, once shiva came to an end Simon's parents kindly invited us for a Friday night dinner, so Mum didn't have to cook. Yet cruelly, no sooner had we got Mum into the car and driven away, than burglars broke in and ransacked her home. They must have been watching the place.

We didn't stay out long but by the time we got back, the thieves had taken everything. All Dad's personal things that Mum wanted to keep as momentos, were stolen. Even Dad's ring, which we'd hidden inside a concealed dressing table light – the safest place we could think of - had vanished. Mum was heartbroken.

That was bad enough but then, a week later, the weather turned exceptionally cold. There was a heavy snowfall and Mum's roof caved in. Worse, when the snow thawed, the melting water flooded the place.

Fortunately, Simon and I had moved to a larger, family home not far from our maisonette in Stanmore before James was born. And thank goodness we did. It meant that when disaster struck, at least we were able to rescue Mum and bring her straight over to our spare room. She ended up staying with us for months while her house was dried out and repaired. But obviously she was very upset. First she'd lost her husband, then all his things and now the home they'd shared for so many years was ruined. It must have seemed like her life was falling to pieces.

I tried to comfort her but at the same time I was struggling to cope with baby James. My gorgeous son seemed to suffer endless stomach upsets. He'd start crying, draw up his tiny legs and then launch into this terrible projectile vomiting. I'd have to clean him up, change his clothes, calm his distress and then his next feed was due and the whole cycle would start all over again. It was exhausting. Eventually, after much worry and many consultations he was put on a special diet, avoiding cow's milk which seemed to soothe things, but at the time it was just more chaos and stress.

I went through the new mum motions, attending clinics and joining baby groups but once again I didn't fit in. The other mums seemed so happy and fulfilled with just their beautiful babies to think about, but I couldn't share their mood. I'd given birth and lost my father in the same week. There I was, struggling with grief for my dad, as well as caring for my grieving mother, organising the rebuilding of her wrecked house and learning to cope with a tiny boy who couldn't seem to stomach any of the food I gave him.

What should have been blissful early months had more of a stressful quality for me. Yet looking back, I wonder now if maybe the apparent disasters weren't such disasters at all. Could the spirit world have arranged things so mum had no choice but to come and be looked after during those first weeks of loss?

Which also meant she was on hand to help me adjust to motherhood? All in all, in an odd way, perhaps our misfortunes weren't so unfortunate after all.

At the time of course I didn't see it like that. I had no idea about the mysterious way our guardian angels can work. I put the events down to an unbelievable run of bad luck. Yet even then, though I was deaf to whatever the spirit world was trying to tell me, I couldn't help sensing something unseen lurking beneath ordinary, everyday activities and even our most enjoyable celebrations.

On one occasion Simon and I were invited to a swanky wedding at a castle in Ireland. Castle Leslie was a lovely place and it had its share of celebrity guests so I was excited to get the chance to experience it.

We'd booked for one night with the option of extending our stay and as we approached up the drive we could see it was impressive. The Castle itself had been rebuilt in Victorian times I believe, but it was set in a 17th century estate, with 1,000 acres of rolling green grounds and several lakes. It was absolutely beautiful. Yet for some reason, as we walked up to the front door I was overcome with a horrible feeling of dread.

'I can't go in,' I said to Simon.

'What d'you mean you can't go in?'

'I can't,' I said, shrinking back from the big entrance door.

'Something bad happened here.'

Simon sighed. He'd had this problem with me before. He couldn't forget a recent holiday we'd shared with family in Florence, Italy. We were doing the rounds of the glorious mediaeval churches to admire the frescoes. Most were lovely but unfortunately, there were others that had an alarming effect on me. My feet would come to an abrupt stop at the huge wooden doors and I could not enter. I felt violently sick.

It was puzzling. They were holy places and quite magnificent from what I could see from the doorway. Yet I felt as if some terrible, tragic event had taken place there. I was ill just contemplating going inside. In the end the others took the tour while Simon and I went shopping.

Now here it was again.

'Look, we've got to go in,' said Simon, getting exasperated and who can blame him, 'We've booked, and we're guests at the wedding and they're expecting us! Come on, it'll be fine.'

And he took my arm and walked me briskly inside. We were shown up to a room at the top of the building, with a four poster bed and wood panelling. It was lovely – but I didn't like it. Straight away I noticed an old portrait on the wall with eyes that followed you round the room and for some reason I got the strong impression this chamber had once been a nursery.

Nevertheless, I managed to change into my wedding outfit and we enjoyed the ceremony which took place at a picturesque chapel in the grounds. But later that night, after the wedding breakfast was cleared away- we got chatting in the bar to the man who owned the castle. He told us the place was renowned for being haunted.

'See,' I said to Simon, 'Told you so!'

That night I just couldn't get to sleep. I tossed and turned in that big four poster, all the time aware of a male presence in the room. He was not threatening in any way but I felt a strong sense of sadness that was very unsettling.

The next morning, after a hasty breakfast, we declined the offer to stay another night and made our escape through those lush green grounds. And as the sunlit castle dwindled away in the rear view mirror, I felt as if a huge weight had been lifted off my shoulders.

It was such a puzzling experience that when we got home, I did some research on Castle Leslie. I was amazed to discover the castle was described as being haunted by amongst others, the spirit of Norman Leslie – heir to the estate - who was sadly killed in 1914 at the Battle of Armentieres during World War 1.

Apparently young Norman led a brave charge on the German guns, armed only with a sword. Poor Norman didn't stand a chance of course. He was cut down almost immediately and his splendid sword, which had been presented to him by Queen Victoria's third son, Prince Arthur, on Norman's graduation from Sandhurst Military Academy, was lost in the churning mud.

That might have been the end of the story except for an astonishing postscript. Eighteen years later, in the 1930s, the farmer who now owned the former battlefield was out ploughing, when a flash of silver caught his eye. He went to investigate and found himself pulling a hefty sword out of the soil. Prince Arthur's engraved inscription to Norman Leslie was still legible and so the sword ended up being returned to Castle Leslie – where it remains to this day.

How amazing, I thought when I finished reading the story. Could it have been Norman I sensed in our splendid bedroom that night, or one of the other spirits associated with the castle? Too late to find out now.

These days I was concentrating on being a full-time mum. Simon was doing well at work and I had quite enough to do caring for James without thinking of finding another job. I'd never been ambitious and was happy enough to go with the flow and be a home-maker. But then one day Lorraine invited me to new diet club she'd found in a nearby suburb. I was always eager to shed a bit of baby weight, so Mum offered to look after James while I went along to the club with Lorraine to pick up some tips.

It turned out we'd stumbled across a branch of Slimming World, now a household name but then, not well known in our area. We sat there enthralled, watching the dieters being weighed and listening to a talk by the woman who ran the branch. It sounded wonderful the way she described it. There was no calorie counting and the food you could eat was a revelation. Lots of smoked salmon and meat and tasty treats. Definitely my kind of diet I thought. Bring it on!

'Hey... you could do that Bev,' whispered Lorraine when the branch manager had finished speaking. 'Why don't you apply for a job?'

'Me?' I said in surprise. 'You're joking! I couldn't stand up there in front of all those people.'

I was always the girl who hid at the back of the class at school and lived in fear of being called upon to read out loud. The terror of making a mistake and looking a fool made my cheeks burn and my mouth dry up just thinking about it.

'Yes you could,' she insisted.

I laughed it off. The idea was quite horrifying. Completely wrong for me. What was Lorraine thinking of? She knew I was incredibly shy.

Yet back home a few days later, as I tucked into my Slimming World meal and thought again what a good diet it was, a voice said: 'You should do this. It would be good for you.'

I looked round. James was asleep. Mum was back in Edgware. There was no one there. I didn't even have the radio on.

'You should do it,' the voice said again.

I wasn't looking for a job and I had plenty to occupy myself, yet somehow I felt as if I ought to do what the voice said. At least give it a try. Nothing will come of it, I reassured myself as I applied to the company. They'll turn me down and that will be that. But at least that voice – my conscience or whatever it was, can't complain if I go through the motions.

Yet surprisingly, Slimming World didn't turn me down. It was a franchise and they seemed to think it would suit me. I was given a thorough training. I hired a church hall as they advised, not far from mum's home in Edgware, I posted flyers and on the appointed day, drove to the hall expecting maybe a couple of curious, slightly overweight people to wander through the door to see what was going on.

Everything was quiet as I put out the chairs, so I sat myself down at a table and began sorting out the paperwork while I waited to greet anyone who ventured in. To my amazement, when I looked up, fifty-two budding dieters of all shapes and sizes were lined up in front of me. The line just kept on coming. I was gob-smacked as they filed by. This area was clearly crying out for a Slimming World that was for sure. Who'd have thought it? The mysterious voice was right.

Slightly dazed, I went into training mode. I handed out application forms and pens and got them settled on chairs, as I'd been taught to do. But after a while I noticed the cheerful buzz in the hall had subsided a few decibels and they were looking at me expectantly.

This was the bit where I was supposed to stand up and address the audience I realised with horror. I stared out at the fifty-two faces staring back at me and my mouth went dry, my knees went weak and my stomach started doing somersaults.

I can't! I thought, hanging back near the wall. This is all a dreadful mistake. But the next second a strong hand placed itself on the small of my back and a great shove propelled me right out in front of the audience.

'Uh…Hello, ladies and gentleman…' I gabbled, staggering slightly to regain my balance. I looked over my shoulder.

There was no one there. So who pushed me? No time to wonder now. 'Thank you for coming...' I went on, 'I expect... you're wondering...' and suddenly words were rushing out of my mouth. I'm not even sure what I said but somehow, some part of me seemed to know exactly what to say.

After that the rest of the session flowed like a dream. By the end of it my new clients assured me they'd be back next week.

As I stacked the chairs away after they'd gone I felt exhausted but oddly euphoric. I'd actually stood up there and given a sort of lecture. I never ever dreamed I could do such a thing. I could hardly believe it. I was shy Bev...how on earth did I manage it? Plus, I was now officially a Slimming World consultant.

What's more I seemed to have acquired a golden touch. The next week seventy-five prospective slimmers arrived at the church hall and the week after that there were over a hundred.

As more and more people wanted to join, I eventually had to put on three sessions a week to fit them all in.

And still that voice urged me on. 'Make some recipes.' 'Take some food,' it whispered. I couldn't make out if it was outside my head or inside. Was it just me, talking to myself? Was I going slightly crazy? I just couldn't tell.

Yet the suggestions were good ideas. I fell into the habit of making tasty, but allowable treats to take along to sessions for my clients to try so they could experience how appetizing this 'diet food' could be. I made special quiches and cheesecakes, chopped liver and chocolate cookies. There seemed to be a new inspiration every week.

Soon my Slimming World group were hurrying through their weigh-ins to head to the table where the free food was laid out. They'd spend a companionable hour munching and listening to the talk and then go home clutching the recipes for the snacks they'd just tried.

The idea caught on so fast that a few months later at one of our Slimming World conferences, I was declared best new consultant of the season, and won a trip to Amsterdam!

Everything went well for a couple of years. The unseen voice continued to prompt me with suggestions: 'Make cakes this week.' Or 'Something savoury now.' Usually I obeyed, but sometimes I didn't feel I could.

On one occasion a very big guy appeared in the queue for the weigh-in. 'Don't let him stand on the scales.' The voice said. But how could I refuse? It would have looked so rude. I didn't want to humiliate the poor man, so I ignored the voice and stood back as he stepped onto the scales. There was a quiet but long and ominous creak from beneath his feet as his hefty bulk settled, then the numbers started going wild. He was well over 20 stone – how much over it was impossible to say as the machine gave up the ghost at that point and refused to record another pound.

No one else could be weighed that session. I had to apologise to the group and give them their money back. A new set of scales had to be rushed to the hall for the following week. I should have listened to that voice after all!

It was an enjoyable job though and I'd probably have continued for years had I not become pregnant with our second child. I suffered a lot of sickness with this pregnancy and resting was difficult enough with a lively toddler to run around after. But when my Slimming World work followed me home on top, it became too exhausting.

One of the great things about the plan as far as my clients were concerned was that they could phone me at any time during office hours and evenings for advice and support. Naturally they took advantage of this service, and of course the more clients joined the sessions, the more phone calls I received. Trouble was, I was trying to potty train James at this point and of course the phone would choose to ring at the most inconvenient moments.

'It's very urgent,' insisted one woman as I stood there, potty in one hand, squirming small boy under my arm, 'I'm making sausages for my family and I don't know whether I can have them too.'

'There's this recipe for chicken soup,' said another, 'but it's got lokschen (a type of vermicelli) in it. Am I allowed to eat lockschen?'

Worse were the misunderstandings.

When I rang one new member to see how she was getting on with the eating plan. I was taken aback to find she wasn't happy at all.

'It's my first week and I have to say how disgusted I am with you!' said an angry voice.

'I'm sorry to hear that,' I said, craning my head to see where James had dashed off to. 'What's wrong?'

'How dare you!' she went on, 'How dare you put out a recipe for prawn curry! Prawns are not Kosher!'

'I know,' I said, puzzled, 'But they don't have to be. This isn't a Jewish club – it's for all religions. There are lots of recipes. You just choose the ones that are right for you.'

'Well I think it's disgusting,' she said and slammed the phone down.

In the end it all got too much. Fortunately, inspired by our success in Edgware, Lorraine had decided to try her luck with Slimming World too and opened her own branch in nearby Golders Green. She was doing very well and was quite happy to take over my clients while I went off on an extended 'maternity leave'.

Privately, I wasn't intending to go back. I sensed my consultant days were an interesting interlude but not the main event somehow. It's only now it strikes me they were simply a necessary step along the way. Thanks to Slimming World, I learned for the first time how to conquer my crippling shyness and speak in front of a crowd. Lessons that would prove invaluable later on.

I was able to rest a little more once I said goodbye to my dieting groups and the rest of the pregnancy went well. Rachel turned out to be a lovely, mid-summer baby, born 23rd June. Yet once again the actual birth wasn't straight forward. I'd been hoping for a natural birth second time around but the consultant told me I needed another caesarean.

This was disappointing, particularly for Simon so we went for a second opinion – I'd so wanted him to see his baby being born. Yet the second doctor agreed with the first. A caesarean it had to be.

Unfortunately, though we didn't realise it, there was a misunderstanding about the instructions I was given on the subject of eating before the operation. I ended up eating solid food too close to the anaesthetic I was told later and as a result, nearly died on the operating table.

'You went blue,' the nurse said when I eventually came round after a worryingly long delay, 'we nearly lost you.'

Yet the drama passed me by completely. All I remember was being surrounded by light: lovely warm, bright light. I felt quite relaxed, quite comfortable, no anxiety, no pain, I was just floating gently in this wonderful sea of light. To be honest I was in no hurry to come back.

When I finally opened my eyes a day later, Simon was standing by the bed, our little daughter in his arms. I couldn't hold her yet, I was still too weak but I could see she had lots of silky dark hair, deep blue eyes and she was quite gorgeous in every way.

My ecstatic Mum had even been in and put a cute little baby hair-band topped with a pink bow round her downy head so she looked even prettier.

And how lovely to have a little girl, I thought, smiling woozily. All those pretty dresses and sparkly shoes I can treat her to. I could hardly wait.

SEVEN:

'You've just described my dead husband...'

The room was very warm, and soporific, meditation-type music gently filled the quiet space. It had been droning on for quite a while now and to be frank, it was getting boring.

My back was starting to ache on the firm, dining-room chair and I shifted surreptitiously. How much longer could this go on? I allowed my eyelashes to lift a fraction, and peeped discreetly round the table. The rest of the group were all sitting there, eyes closed, feet firmly planted on the floor, blissful expressions on their faces. Well they were all clearly 'getting it' but nothing was happening for me. I shut my eyes again and tried to concentrate. But no. Nothing. Just darkness.

I thought back to the medium I'd visited a few years before. The one who told me I should join a development circle. Well here I was, sitting in a circle just as she advised and it was doing nothing for me at all.

Oddly enough, this particular visit wasn't even my idea. It was my sister-in-law Sarah who'd heard of the group and thought it might be interesting for us to join them for a session. As she suggested it, the words of the medium in the cluttered house bounced suddenly into my mind. I hadn't thought of her advice for years but hey! Who knew what went on at those evenings? It could be an interesting experience.

'Ok,' I said to Sarah, 'I'd love to go.'

A few days later we'd arrived at the address Sarah had been given and found ourselves outside a modern, purpose-built block of flats on the edge of town. A dozen or so perfectly normal looking men and women were heading inside so we tagged on the end and followed them into the flat.

Our instructress, a middle aged, dark haired woman in a smart dress was standing in the hallway ushering us along. She seemed a little harassed but did her best to welcome us all. Perhaps there were more of us than she'd expected.

Just inside the door I noticed a man sitting in an armchair. He was wearing a colourful paisley smoking jacket and carpet slippers and made no move to head into the séance room with the others, so I guessed he must live there. He gave me a sympathetic smile as I passed. Almost as if he was thinking: 'Rather you than me, girl!'

Anyway I did my best. Our psychic-medium instructor welcomed Sarah and me and found us a place round the big, circular table. Then she explained she was going to put on some music to help us relax and we should follow her in our minds, as she took us on a mental journey through a beautiful waterfall of colours. We needed to plant our feet firmly on the carpet to ground ourselves, she said, then we should close our eyes, let our imagination wander and see what happened. We may see pictures, she went on, or receive impressions. We might even hear voices. Afterwards we'd compare notes and talk through what the spirit world had sent.

Simple enough instructions of course but I found them oddly difficult to follow. My mind wandered alright, but not onto spiritual matters. I couldn't seem to picture the waterfall she was talking about. Instead my thoughts strayed to little Rachel, now an energetic toddler. All my baby girl's dark hair had gradually changed colour and these days she was an exquisite blonde. I hoped she was behaving for the babysitter. And James of course. He could be a handful. So intelligent and lively, chances are he wouldn't want to go to sleep. I did hope they'd be good.

And still the music and the words wound on. Was there no end to it? But finally to my relief, I realised the medium had ceased speaking and the music was getting slower and softer until mercifully, it died away altogether. One by one the circle blinked their eyes open. Some of them appeared to have returned from a long way off. Others were apparently overwhelmed by the visions they'd seen.

Our hostess went round the table encouraging them to share their experiences. Some were fairly interesting. They'd seen lovely colours or felt very peaceful. But others saw all manner of unusual objects or scenes. Some reckoned they'd even met their guides.

I stared at them in amazement. I felt such a failure. 'I got nothing,' I confessed in disappointment when the medium reached me. 'I didn't see anything. Just darkness. Just what you normally get when you close your eyes.'

'Don't worry Beverley, it takes time,' the medium said kindly, 'Did you feel anything, no matter how small… maybe you noticed something a little bit unusual…?'

'No,' I said.

'You must have seen something.'

I started to shake my head, then something struck me. Now I came to think about it, there was something a bit unusual, not in this room but outside. The man sitting by the door. I couldn't quite put my finger on it but he seemed a little out of place somehow.

'The only thing I can think of wasn't in here,' I said, 'It was out in the other room – the man sitting on the armchair by the door.'

'What man?' asked the medium.

'The one in the paisley smoking jacket and carpet slippers,' I said. Everyone looked at me blankly.

The medium peered at me more closely. 'Go on…' she said.

So I described him as best I could.

'You've just described my husband, and that was his favourite chair and he always wore that jacket when he was relaxing,' said the medium, 'But he died six months ago.'

Now it was the rest of the group who were astounded. It turned out no one else had seen a man sitting in the armchair. There was no one in the flat but us. They stared at me open mouthed.

'Wow!' whispered Sarah, 'Did you really see him?'

'Clear as day!' I whispered back, just as puzzled as she was.

'Don't worry about not getting anything in the meditation dear,' said the medium, recovering from her surprise. 'It takes time. You've got potential. I'm sure it will improve as you go along.'

Until that moment I'd been thinking it wasn't worth my going back but if I'd really seen her late husband, maybe I should give the circle another chance.

So the following week Sarah and I returned to the block of flats. We sat through another meditation where once again I saw nothing. I did get my shopping list for the next few days sorted out in my head though! But then the medium decided to try a different exercise.

On the sideboard next to the table she'd put a big bowl stacked with various random items – pieces of jewellery and assorted trinkets. Now she brought the bowl over and asked us all to choose an object and hold it in our hands.

This was called 'psychometry' she explained. We might be able to sense something about the owner of the object simply by touching it.

'Just keep it in your hand for a minute or two, concentrate and see what impressions you pick up,' she said.

Everyone helped themselves. I dug my fingers in and found they'd immediately closed around a chunky ring. I knew instantly it belonged to the medium's husband. This is too weird I thought, after last week's episode, and I went to put it back. But the medium wouldn't let me.

'No you've picked it,' she said, 'You've got to keep what you first chose.'

Oh well, I thought. She'll just have to put up with weird. Yet once again I didn't get any impressions. It was just her husband's ring. Round the table we went again, with most of the other students coming out with interesting details about their items which the medium declared to be accurate.

Then she came to me. After the man in the chair episode she was clearly expecting something.

I shook my head. 'Nothing much,' I said, 'I think this belongs to the man I saw last week, your husband…' But instead of finishing there as I intended, more words were forming in my mouth and they were determined to speak themselves. I could hear my voice – describing the medium's husband by the sound of it - the sentences pouring out, but I had no control of what I was saying. I was dimly aware the others were staring at me in a startled way but I couldn't help it and I couldn't stop. Then after a while the flow seemed to slow, then stop and I came to a halt.

Everything had gone very quiet. I glanced at the medium. She seemed shocked.

'You've just recited the exact words that were spoken at my husband's eulogy,' she said in a shaken voice. 'And yes, that is his ring.'

I put the ring down, shocked myself. How did that happen?

This particular circle was getting a bit unsettling I thought. Something was happening with me, that's for sure, but not the things the medium intended. It was happening so quickly. I felt a little out of control and it made me nervous. I sensed the medium didn't quite know what to do with me either. It would probably be best all round if I tried a different group. Maybe finding the right circle was a bit like finding the right hairdresser or therapist – you just had to find the one that resonated with you.

So for the next few years I joined a number of circles close to my home and I began to gain more understanding. The more I practised the more I too could see pictures during meditations and I often picked up impressions when I held objects donated for psychometry. I learned the basics of mediumship and how to connect with my guide and how to give readings.

It was an intriguing interest but nothing more at that stage. Real life was my children, growing fast and busy with school and my marriage. Simon was doing very well at work. He climbed the ladder at his original firm, was then head-hunted for another and ended up as managing director of a successful property company.

At one point he was working in Canary Wharf, Docklands and I agreed to move out to Essex which was easier for his commute. There was nothing wrong with our new home but I missed being so close to Mum and my old friends. We were only 25 miles away but I felt uprooted. Nevertheless I got into the habit of picking Mum up once a week so we could spend the day together.

I was very fortunate that unlike some husbands I'd heard of, Simon didn't resent or mock my interest in spiritual matters.

In fact, like his sister Sarah, he was intrigued too. So much so, he said he'd be happy to have a reading from one of the great mediums my friends kept raving about. She was particularly talented I told him. Simon had always wanted to see if he could contact his late grandparents – he'd been so fond of them – so he said ok, maybe I could arrange something.

Delighted with his enthusiasm, I set about organising the reading. The first appointment she could offer was the late afternoon of February 9 1996. The 9th was a Friday – our traditional family dinner night, but she was a busy lady. If I didn't take the 9th it could be weeks before we could get another appointment I realised, so I accepted.

'Oh can't she make it a different day?' Simon said when I told him, 'I've got a meeting that afternoon.'

Typical, I thought. There was always something.

'No she can't Simon,' I said, a little peeved. 'That's the only space she's got for weeks. Can't you rearrange your meeting?'

He wasn't pleased, but he did.

February 9th arrived and Simon left work early as agreed, came home to change and then set off for the medium's house, a short drive away. Apparently the session went well. Simon was given some fascinating evidence which made him think. He got back time for dinner too. I was very pleased as we gathered round the table and lit the candles. A proper Friday night family meal.

Then the phone rang.

'I'll get it,' said Simon. He went out to the landline but he was gone ages. Work again! I thought crossly. But when he returned his face was ashen. Literally ashen.

'What's wrong?' I asked in alarm as he walked in. He looked terrible.

'There's been a bomb!' he said, shocked. 'Just up the road from the office. All the windows have blown in…I don't think any of our staff are hurt but they don't know yet…'

It turned out the IRA had detonated a huge truck bomb in Docklands. Two people were killed, over 100 were injured, some severely, and there was £150 million worth of damage to the surrounding buildings. The bomb was so powerful it blasted a crater 32ft wide and 10 ft deep in the street.

Had Simon stayed in the area for his intended meeting he could have been injured or even killed. Once again it seemed, the spirit world was looking out for us.

Fortunately, nobody in Simon's company was hurt and they soon recovered from the shock. Business returned to normal. Time passed and Simon continued to thrive professionally. Little by little we became a successful family.

Yet I still hankered after being close to mum. In the end Simon agreed to move some of the way back towards Edgware and we bought a brand new home in a Hertfordshire town, barely twenty-minute drive away.

Simon treated us too, to a flat in Spain and we began attending glamorous functions related to his business. Through his work we were invited to Wimbledon and

Henley Regatta, Ascot and Cheltenham races and no end of dinner dances at London's poshest hotels and dinner parties in lavish private houses.

Simon also became involved with fund raising for Norwood, a children's charity. This led to us attending even more swanky events. Soon we were mixing with the rich and stylish and rubbing shoulders with celebrities.

Coming out of the ladies at one dinner I bumped into Simon – the X Factor – Cowell. I happened to be phoning home at that moment trying to persuade Rachel to do her homework. Rachel was besotted with Simon that point in her life so without thinking, as soon as I realised who was standing in front of me, I thrust the phone at the surprised Mr Cowell.

'You couldn't tell my daughter to do her homework could you?' I said, 'She'd listen to you!'

Simon grinned. 'What's her name?' he asked taking the phone.

'Rachel,' I said.

'Rachel,' he said into the phone, 'This is Simon Cowell. How are you? I'm here with your mum. I would like you to go and do your homework!'

She did too. Nice man, Mr Cowell. And of course Rachel's street cred shot sky high when she got back to school.

We also became friends with the late TV presenter Jeremy Beadle who spent a lot of time fund-raising for some of the same charities as Simon. Jeremy was a great practical joker and he was always phoning the house, pretending to be someone else, and asking to speak to Simon.

'I know it's you Jeremy,' I used to say hearing Mrs Doubtfire on the phone again. 'I recognise your voice now. That fake accent's rubbish!'

And he'd burst out laughing.

From the outside it must have looked as if we enjoyed the most wonderful life. As I swished into the car in my latest glitzy evening dress, sparkly shoes on my feet off to yet another exclusive dinner, the neighbours must have thought I was the luckiest woman in town. Yet the truth was, I wasn't happy. Apart from a few genuinely warm and kind people, most of our new acquaintances struck me as rather shallow and insincere. Nothing seemed real. They were more interested in what you had and where you lived, than who you were.

At first glance, the women I met were gorgeous. Intimidatingly beautiful. Perfect hair, perfect make-up, perfect designer clothes, perfect figures, perfect boobs, perfect marriages. Yet often in their elegant company I felt so bored. The only topic of conversation seemed to be how well their children were doing at their expensive private schools, where they were going on their next exotic holidays or the latest offering from Louis Vuitton and Chanel. Is it me? I used to wonder, as I fell more and more silent over some delectable cordon bleu meal. The food was divine yet the evening turned so dreary I could scream!

And when I got to know them better I discovered that behind many a glossy façade, it was all fake. Their faces were only perfect thanks to overpriced cosmetics, their figures through abstaining from that glorious food and the perfect marriages were only perfect in photographs.

When she discovered I'd learned to read tarot, one of these exquisite creatures begged me to read for her. To my surprise, I saw at once that all in the garden was not as rosy as she made out.

'Things don't look too happy at home,' I ventured as tactfully as I could.

She sighed. She didn't like to admit it but this was obviously why she'd come.

'I want to know what to do about my husband,' she said at last, 'He's so awful to me. I hate him! I'd like to stab his eyes out.'

Slightly shocked, I passed her the cards. 'I can't give you advice,' I said, 'I can only tell you what the cards say. Then it's up to you to make your own decision.'

She nodded impatiently and we got started. As I recall, the cards seemed to suggest the relationship was stormy and she'd probably be better off making a big break. They badly needed to talk if they were to have any hope of saving the marriage. Without some big changes on her husband's part, there was unlikely to be a happy outcome.

'Too right,' she said grimly as she swept out at the end. 'I'll make that ****** pay…'

Oh dear I thought. We won't be seeing that couple together at the next dinner.

Yet a couple of weeks later I opened OK magazine and was staggered to see on the diary page, a picture of that same, husband-hating acquaintance, snuggled up to the loathed man, beaming as if they were the most loved up couple in London.

'I can't leave him,' she admitted the next time we met, 'How would I manage?'

I was astonished. If she hated him, how could she bear to stay? Little did I realise I was to meet a lot more like her and her reaction wasn't uncommon.

On another occasion we were invited for a holiday on a yacht in the South of France. Gorgeously tanned couples drifted around in designer beachwear and an artistic tea was laid out in the shade.

'Oo Bev, I'd love one of those cakes!' said the slender beauty standing beside me. She was looking longingly at a tray of dainty little confections, all cream and piled raspberries. No more than one bite apiece.

'Well have one,' I said.

'Oh no I couldn't.' She turned away, but the lure of the cakes seemed to draw her back. She stared at them. 'I really, really want one of those cakes!'

I looked at her properly then. She was as thin as my little finger.

'Go on. Treat yourself,' I encouraged mischievously. 'They're only tiny.'

I could see some sort of internal struggle going on behind

her eyes. Then her perfectly manicured hand shot out, she seized a cake and began to nibble it guiltily.

I turned away to fetch my own cake at that point and by the time I turned back, she was gone. But on the table sat her abandoned plate – half a cake lying dejectedly in the middle.

Minute and delicious as they were, and slim as she was, the poor woman could allow herself no more than a tiny bite. So what could I do? I finished it off for her!

In my mind I christened these new acquaintances the 'plastics'. All putting in such a huge effort to project an image that wasn't necessarily them at all. Is it worth it? I wondered. I could see right through them.

Yet Simon didn't share my qualms. He seemed much more comfortable with the plastic set than I did. I didn't fit in with the women but Simon was able to bridge the gap with the men.

One evening we went for a meal with a new colleague of Simon's. This man was seriously wealthy it appeared and Simon seemed to expect me to be impressed.

Afterwards, on the way home in the car he asked if I'd enjoyed the evening.

'Not really,' I said truthfully, 'All he did was go on and on about his plane and which new boat to buy…Why can't we just talk about things that matter in life rather than material things?'

But Simon hadn't minded at all. He enjoyed his new friend's company and was probably a little bit impressed by his lifestyle.

'Just boys' toys!' I said wearily, 'And he went on and on about nothing else. To be honest I was bored.'

Simon didn't say anything. It was obvious we were going in different directions.

EIGHT:

A big, dark shadow of a man shot through the window into the room...

'Bev!' said Simon as he emerged from the basement, a puzzled look on his face. 'Why do you keep opening the cupboard door?'

'I don't!' I said. I knew which cupboard he meant. It was just after we moved into our brand new house in Hertfordshire which came with a large, very handy basement complete with a nice big cupboard. We nicknamed it the 'Costco Cupboard' because it was ideal for storing bulk buys of cleaning materials and toilet rolls. Plus old china and broken toasters and things we didn't want to throw away because I'm a bit of a hoarder. 'I'm always closing it. Why do *you* keep leaving it open?'

'I don't,' said Simon, '*I'm* always closing it. I come and close it every day.'

'But so do I!' We stared at each other, bewildered. Every morning after Simon had gone to work I went into the basement and found the cupboard door wide open. So, tutting to myself, I would close it.

Turned out most evenings after he got home, Simon also popped into the basement. And he too found the cupboard wide open. And no doubt tutting to himself, he also closed it – wondering in passing, why I seemed to need so many cleaning products every day. I mean a clean house was one thing but this was getting ridiculous.

Until that moment, we'd both thought the other one was responsible – but it had seemed too trivial to mention.

'Maybe it's a faulty catch,' said Simon when we realised neither of us was the culprit, because he always made sure it was properly closed every time he shut it. He was that sort of person.

So he went down to the basement and spent a while fiddling with the lock and opening and closing the door. Nope, nothing wrong. The cupboard shut perfectly and jiggling or rattling at the handle had no effect. The door remained firmly closed.

After that we got a little obsessed with the cupboard. We checked it frequently. And just about every time we looked, the door was open, no matter how many times we closed it and then left it to its own devices.

Then we noticed that a piece of modern artwork festooned with tiny light bulbs that we'd hung on the wall would keep spontaneously turning on, no matter how many times we switched it off. Could it have been the vibration of our feet or another mystery?

I became more and more intrigued. We were the first occupants of the house so surely we couldn't blame some spirit connected with previous owners? There were no previous owners!

I had to admit though, much as I liked the house, there was something faintly unusual about the place. I was only aware of it at night when I went to bed. I'd wake up suddenly, with the feeling other people had just come into the room, though I couldn't see them. Or I'd open my eyes and feel as if I was floating; other times I'd wake to see a swirl of colours in the darkness that gradually faded as I watched and then disappeared. It wasn't frightening, just odd.

I'd joined a couple of local development circles since we moved in, so one day as I came back yet again from shutting the cupboard door, I picked up the phone and called a medium who'd been recommended by one of my new friends for advice.

'Walk me round the house,' she said on the other end of the line, 'I can probably pick up what's going on over the phone.'

So, holding the phone out in front of me, I did a little tour of the house. Most of the rooms appeared to be quite neutral and had no effect on the medium, but when we got to the bedroom – the room where I often experienced that weirdly interrupted sleep, she got me to stop. She'd picked up something unusual. 'There's a portal behind the bed,' she said.

I didn't quite understand this but I took it to mean that it was a kind of invisible doorway between the two worlds that unseen spirits could use to enter via the room.

'They sense you're aware of them,' she said, 'They're trying to attract your attention.'

Well they were certainly succeeding, I thought. I'd much

prefer they let me sleep though.

We moved on again and all was unremarkable until we arrived on the stairs to the basement. The medium got me to stand still once more. There was something definite here.

'I'm picking up a woman. No, *two* women,' she corrected herself, 'They were killed…in a fire. They were kitchen maids in an old manor many years ago.'

'But this is a new house!' I reminded her, 'It's never caught fire.'

'Doesn't make any difference if the house is new,' the medium went on. 'It's the land it stands on. There was some sort of fire on this spot a long, long time ago and both these women died.'

'Well what do they want now?' I asked.

'They think you can help them,' said the medium, 'That's why they keep opening the cupboard door. They're trying to attract your attention, just like the others upstairs.'

The way she described it, unknown to Simon and I, our house must have been pretty crowded. He'd never believe it if I told him I thought.

'Don't worry we can sort it out together,' said the medium. She explained they needed to cross over into the spirit world. Little did I know this would be my first experience of helping them find their families on the other side. I should try to visualise a very bright light and imagine a warm, loving feeling flowing out from the light. 'Now in your mind, tell the women to walk towards the light. To go to the light.

Encourage them to walk right into the light.'

I shut my eyes and concentrated. After a moment or two I managed to conjure up an image of a beautiful light – a bit like the light I'd seen when my dad was so ill – and I asked the unknown women to walk towards it. Were they listening? Who could tell? I kept repeating the suggestion: 'Go to the light, go to the light. Your families are waiting for you.' And then all of a sudden I got the impression of movement. Almost as if two shadows had passed across my vision – and then they were gone. The light dimmed.

'It's ok. They've crossed to the world of spirit! Well done,' said the medium.

I opened my eyes. Was that it? The medium assured me it was.

'I don't think you'll have any more problems,' she said, 'but just give me a call if you do.'

After I put the phone down, I stood there in the silence, trying to gauge the atmosphere. Was it my imagination or did the house feel different already?

It certainly seemed as if it did, to me. There was a lighter quality to the air, as if a subtle heaviness had just melted away like mist in the sun. Funny, I'd never noticed that slightly sombre feel before, until it was gone. I looked at the cupboard. The door was closed. It stared blankly back at me as if to say: 'Well what d'you expect? I'm a cupboard.'

I didn't trust it though. Several times throughout the afternoon I dashed down to the basement expecting to catch it out. But no. The door remained firmly closed. And strangely enough, from that day on it remained closed – except for when we opened it deliberately – ever after.

The medium obviously knew what she was doing and her success inspired me to work even harder at the developing circles. Our sessions were becoming more and more interesting. One evening we were meditating as usual and encouraged to connect with our guides. I'd had some success at this by now and often felt the presence of an unseen being just behind my shoulder, but this particular session was different.

All of a sudden the darkness behind my eyes cleared and a figure was standing there – an awe-inspiring knight on a big horse. He seemed to be wearing armour but with a white tunic over the top and in the centre of the tunic was a vivid red cross.

'I am your guide,' he said, 'I will help you on your journey. Now is the time to make myself known to you.'

And then the vision faded and he was gone.

'That's really good,' said our medium teacher when I told her what had happened. 'You've got a strong connection with your guide now. He'll help you every step of the way.'

I was excited but also intrigued by the outfit my guide had worn. When I got home I rushed to do some research. Eventually I came across a picture of a knight in the very same type of costume – a white tunic emblazoned with a stylised cross just like my guide's. The caption explained that this was the uniform of the Knights Templar – also known as the Order of the Solomon's Temple – a controversial Catholic military order that were involved in the crusades.

How I'd ended up with such an impressive helper I couldn't imagine but I was very glad he was there.

Not all the visions I saw were so comforting though. One night I woke up suddenly with the feeling something was very wrong. Instantly wide awake, I sat up to look around and as I did so a big, dark shadow of a man shot through the window into the room. As I watched, it whizzed straight across the bed and seemed to land right on Simon's back.

The next second Simon let out the most blood curdling scream I've ever heard and jolted violently in the bed.

'What is it? What is it?' I cried – though I already knew.

'Get it off me! Get it off me!' he shrieked in genuine terror.

Yet when I bent close to look, there was nothing there. The shadow had vanished. All I could see was Simon struggling. I ran my hand down his back to make sure – nothing physical there at all. Whatever it was had obviously gone.

'It's ok, it's ok,' I soothed. 'You were dreaming.'

Gradually he calmed down. 'There was something on my back,' he said sleepily.

'You were dreaming,' I said, 'Don't worry, I expect it was some big busty blonde coming to visit you. It's ok.'

He seemed to accept it. He smiled dozily at my joke, turned over and a few moments later he was fast asleep again. But that was me spooked because I woke before Simon experienced the figure, before it had woken him up. For the rest of the night, I remained sitting bolt upright, staring at the window until the first light of dawn drove all the shadows away.

I said no more about it to Simon over breakfast. He seemed to have forgotten the incident and as he was clearly unharmed there was no point in worrying him. Yet I remained baffled. I would even have been prepared to put the episode down to a nightmare on Simon's part combined with an overactive imagination and an optical illusion on mine, had it not been for one small postscript.

As it happened later that very morning, Simon had an appointment with a healer. He'd been suffering from a sprained muscle for some time and as he was still enthusiastic about alternative therapies, he'd booked a slot with this well regarded healer he often visited, in the hope of ditching his pain-killers and getting better the natural way.

Typical Simon though, just as he was walking into the healer's office, a business call came through on his mobile. It was important, so he dealt with the query as quickly as he could while strolling through the door, then apologised to the therapist who was waiting for him.

'Sorry about that,' he said turning off the phone, 'I came in with someone!'

The healer eyed him piercingly. 'I know you did,' she said, 'but not just on the phone.'

Simon gave her a puzzled look.

'You did come in with someone,' she said, 'Someone on your back. Come on. Let's get you on the therapy table.'

She took him through to her healing room and ended up working on him for three hours – something that had never happened before. At the end of the session she seemed drained.

'You'll be ok now,' she assured him. 'Whatever was on your back. It's gone.'

And it was true Simon did feel much better. Not just around the painful muscle either. He felt more relaxed and cheerful in general.

'Amazing what a spell of healing can do for you,' he told me later, very pleased the drug free therapy had worked so well.

I didn't say anything. I was amazed alright – but not so much about the wonderful power of healing – it was the fact the healer also 'saw' something unpleasant on his back – despite knowing nothing about the incident in the night. I hadn't been imagining things after all.

So what could that shadow have been? I don't believe in possession or evil spirits, yet something disturbing had happened. True, Simon had a very pressured job and was always worrying about some project or other. No doubt he often had 'difficult' people 'on his back'. Could it be that while he slept, his pent up stress had taken on a tangible form? Could his own anxious energy have been released while he dreamed, and ricocheted round the room like a dark shadow before returning to its owner?

We'll never know I suppose, but it made me wonder.

Out in our everyday world, we were still often socialising with 'the plastics' as I continued to call them and though I tried really hard to fit in, their company frequently made me uneasy. Often we'd be going out for dinner at the latest gastro-pub and I'd leave home, comfortable but smart I felt, in my nicest trousers and top. Off we'd go, me feeling I looked quite ok until we walked into the pub and some glossy vision in designer dress, sky-scraper heels and perfect make-up, would unwind herself languidly from a barstool and immediately make me feel like a reject from Poundland.

It was quite amazing the effort some of these women put in to look glamorous. Once, flying off on a trip with one of Simon's business associates I was gobsmacked to turn up at the airport for our early morning flight to find the associate's wife, already there. She stood, sipping coffee, diamond earrings dangling almost to her shoulders, jewels flashing from every finger and six inch Louboutin designer heels on her feet.

I watched in amazement as she teetered precariously towards the gate, clutching an oversized piece of hand luggage.

'Wow I have to admire your stamina,' I said looking down at my trainers – was that a new scuff I'd somehow picked up? 'I couldn't walk more than six steps in those.'

She gave a nervous little laugh.

'It makes me feel good to wear these through the airport,' she said. 'I enjoy it.'

I glanced my trainers again, looking even more worn now. Maybe I should make more of an effort! I thought.

The other thing about the glittering events we attended - a great deal of expensive champagne was drunk, and it had a decidedly liberating effect on some of the women. These days the conversation often turned to boob jobs which had become very fashionable and popular amongst this smart set, so this particular evening, after a few glasses of fizz, a certain recently enhanced member of the group decided to warn the gathering of the potential hazards.

Despite the fact she looked stunning in a sparkling, low cut sequinned evening dress that needed no shoulder straps to stay in place, she wasn't happy.

'It's a complete botch,' she slurred, 'That surgeon…he ruined me…ruined me! Made a complete botch. I might sue. Just look what he's done!'

And with that, she yanked down the bodice, in full view of the bar area to reveal two large, bra-less breasts. Sure enough, she was right. The surgery clearly hadn't been a success. The breasts didn't match. Not only in size, but one was looking one way and the other in quite a different direction. The effect was distinctly unsettling.

What the other guests made of it I can't imagine. Fortunately, after much sympathising we managed to persuade her to restore her top, but it was touch and go. She was determined the incompetent surgeon should be named and shamed and she wanted everyone to witness his poor workmanship.

On another occasion, once again in a restaurant where

copious bottles of bubbles had been enjoyed and cosmetic surgery was being discussed, one of the women decided to impress the men with what she considered her 'perfect triangle'. I wasn't sure exactly what she'd had done but she insisted on lifting her skirt to display her knickers and proceeded to parade around the table so that all the appreciative husbands could inspect the marvellous view.

It went down a treat with the men but the women weren't impressed. Especially the party hostess. And the evening had only just begun – hors d'oeuvres hadn't even been served yet! I watched the other wives exchanging unamused glances. That's one lady off the next party list, I couldn't help thinking. If the wives have anything to do with it anyway!

I was taken aback, but joined in the laughter. Yet inside I was thinking: 'Really?' 'Is this how we spend our time…?'

And while I made a few good friends, some of the women could turn surprisingly unfriendly without warning. I remember once arriving a little late for dinner with one particular lady.

'I'm so sorry,' I said as I hurried to the table, 'A girlfriend phoned just as I was leaving, she was dreadfully upset. She's just lost someone close.'

Instead of the understanding smile I was expecting, my companion sighed and rolled her eyes.

'We all have difficult days,' she said sourly, 'It's selfish to be late. I've been having a terrible time too.'

'Oh my god what's wrong?' I asked.

'I've had my daughter on the phone in a terrible state. She's had a row with her boyfriend. Yet *I* managed to be here on time.'

I happened to know that her daughter was all of eleven years old so I couldn't believe the tiff was too tragic.

'Well I'm sorry to hear that,' I muttered, swallowing a lump in my throat at her angry tone, 'but my friend was just bereaved. I had to talk to her.'

My companion sniffed and picked up the menu. 'Well now you're here, what are you going to order?'

It wasn't the most enjoyable dinner I've ever eaten.

No matter how hard I tried I couldn't seem to get on the same wavelength as these people.

One of the worst occasions involved a charity lunch at a smart hotel where a speaker was entertaining the assembled diners with a talk about the Royal Family. I hadn't wanted to go and my intuition was telling me it was a bad idea, but it was for charity after all, they needed the funds so I knew I ought to support them.

Everything went well enough until the speaker turned to the subject of Princess Diana – and not in a good way.

'What sort of person would throw herself down the stairs just to get attention?' said the speaker in what seemed to me a sarcastic voice.

And she preceded to go on about how the princess could be contrary, difficult and change her mind on a sixpence.

Maybe it was because years ago I'd admired Diana and so many people told me at the time I looked like her, that I'd developed an affinity with the Princess, but whatever the reason, I became more and more upset with the tone of the talk and the reaction of the audience who were revelling in the gossip. It struck me as dreadfully disrespectful. In fact, I began to feel increasingly annoyed on Diana's behalf.

At the end the audience was invited to ask questions. There was a barrage of questions from diners, hungry for more-juicy titbits about Diana. Inside I was seething. 'Go on, go on. Put your hand up!' said a little voice inside.

'Shall I?' I wondered, coming over all shy again. 'Is it worth it?'

'Go on, go on! Put your hand up,' prodded the voice again. It was almost as if Diana herself was speaking to me. The next thing I knew my hand shot up, waving so high over all the heads my arm nearly came out of its socket. It's not me doing this I thought vaguely. Each time I was overlooked until finally the speaker announced the last question.

'Yes you, back there in the turquoise dress.' smiled the speaker, nodding at me. She obviously thought I was going to say something complimentary.

I felt myself tipped abruptly out of my chair and I grabbed the table to steady myself on my feet.

'Well, with respect,' I began nervously, staring round at the curious eyes from every table suddenly turned in my direction, '…with respect…Diana isn't here to defend herself. Do you understand about mental illness?'

The speaker looked affronted. 'Of course I do. I have a relative with dementia.'

'But that's not the same,' I persisted, 'I'm talking about depression. You are saying all these things about Diana but she was unwell at the time with depression and now she's not here to defend herself.'

The room had gone deathly quiet. I glanced round the sparkling tables but suddenly everyone was looking the other way. I'd imagined they'd agree with me. I thought I was surely voicing what everyone else was thinking, but apparently not. There was a distinctly hostile feeling in the air – and not towards the speaker.

The silence grew and it was getting embarrassing. Another hand went up uncertainly.

'Yes, we'll make this the last question then!' said the speaker obviously a bit annoyed and relieved to have an excuse to be done with me.

And as the final bland query began to roll, I sat down.

But now my table companions seemed to have disowned me. No one would catch my eye. No one would speak to me. For the rest of the event it was as if I'd become invisible. I couldn't understand it. Here I was in a room full of women, posh Prada handbags stuffed with anti-depressants, yet they couldn't show support for an unhappy young royal who had probably struggled with her mental health.

I was very glad when the whole excruciating lunch finally came to an end and I could escape to my car. Later, back home, something made me take a look at Facebook. Maybe a few of the group had mentioned the lunch? Maybe someone else had voiced an opinion of the talk. I couldn't believe I was the only one who thought the criticism of Diana was unfair.

Sure enough there were already a number of posts about the event but to my horror, as I scrolled down the page I realised the contributors weren't discussing the talk, they were discussing me.

'For someone who's not used to speaking in public,' a fellow guest I knew quite well had written, 'she certainly did a good job of spoiling the event.'

I was mortified. Speaking out for mental health was important to me. But if speaking my mind meant that was the end of invitations to similar functions - it was fine by me.

NINE:

'Every time she speaks, I see sparkles flying around...'

I was in the kitchen when I heard it. There I was, standing at the worktop scrambling some eggs for a family breakfast, when a booming male voice said: 'Go to the Arthur Findlay College.'

I looked round. There was no one there. Simon and the kids were in the other room watching TV. I could hear the faint sounds of music and excitable dialogue wafting through the wall.

These days I was used to invisible voices occasionally giving me a message so I wasn't alarmed. I was puzzled though.

'Go to the Arthur Findlay College,' it said again.

'What's the Arthur Findlay College?' I said out loud.

But frustratingly, there was no reply.

Just to make sure, I zipped into the sitting room. Sure enough my family were all sprawled across the sofa and the carpet watching Saturday morning tv.

'Did anyone call me?' I asked.

Three heads turned vaguely in my direction.

'No,' said Simon.

'Ok. No problem,' I said and went back to the eggs. I'd have to look up this Arthur Findlay place later. That's if it existed at all.

As soon as breakfast was cleared away, I couldn't wait to get to our home office where Simon kept the computer to start to do an online search. Sure enough there really was a place called the Arthur Findlay College and it was based near Stansted airport of all places. It appeared to be a highly unusual establishment. It was for people interested in Spiritualism, healing and mediumship and offered residential training courses on various aspects of these subjects.

Why haven't I heard of this college before? I wondered. Or perhaps I had long ago and forgotten about it? I was no scholar and had never even contemplated going to college at my age, yet somehow it sounded like just my kind of place. It wasn't even that far from where I lived. Easily drivable in an hour.

I chose a course called the Power Within and impulsively phoned the college to book. I knew the voice intended me to act fast.

'I'd like to book a place for this course and I'd like a single en suite room please.'

There was a wry chuckle the other end. 'I'm sorry we've only got shared rooms with no en-suites left,' she said.

I was shocked that in this day and age people were still offerings rooms without private facilities.

'Oh I guess I'll have to leave it then,' I said. It was one thing to go to college on my own but the idea of sharing a room with a stranger without even a bathroom was completely out of my comfort zone.

'Wait a minute dear. Let me go and check something.' She went off then came back and said, 'As it's only a few weeks till the course starts I can let you have a twin room as a single. There's no bathroom but the toilet is just down the hall.'

I took a snap decision it was do-able. Normally I'd mull over decisions like this but I had to pay immediately and within minutes I was committed. But I knew deep inside of me there was no choice to make. When I put the phone down I couldn't help laughing to myself. Wait till my family and friends hear about this. They knew I liked my home comforts.

'Have you ever heard of the Arthur Findlay College?' I asked the medium a couple of days later at my next development circle session.

She nodded. 'Oh yes, I believe it's quite well known. Why?'

'Well I've just booked to go there,' I said, 'It sounds interesting.'

'I wouldn't waste your money dear,' she said, 'I can teach you everything you need to learn anything.'

I felt really slapped down. I'd been so excited. Perhaps she was right, I thought, but for some reason I'd been told to go there. The voice had mentioned the college specifically by name and I knew by now it was better not to ignore the voice.

I didn't argue with my medium mentor, but everything was arranged. James and Rachel were teenagers now, old enough to manage without me for a little while. As for Simon, he enjoyed the odd sporting weekend away with his friends now and then, so I knew he wouldn't complain if I also had an outside interest. He'd probably be pleased. He was quite proud of my developing gifts.

To be honest, almost imperceptibly, Simon and I had been continuing to grow apart. We'd endured a difficult few years despite our outward success. He was caught up in his demanding job and I had been consumed by what seemed like endless family health problems.

First a favourite aunt, my mum's beloved sister had become terminally ill and after a couple of years of bravely suffering, she passed away. Then my sister developed a serious illness requiring a big operation and a lot of ongoing hospital treatment, followed by a long convalescence staying with us. Next Mum had terrible back problems also requiring several surgeries, and in between we discovered James had a worrying back condition that required spinal surgery.

I seemed to spend huge chunks of time ferrying back and forth to an endless stream of hospitals, doing my best to cheer up my sick loved ones while trying to disguise the continual, gnawing anxiety. Hopefully, I was able to comfort them, but by the time I got home after yet another distressing visit I had very little energy left over to be a fun wife to a stressed businessman. I was so used to being strong and everyone's rock, I didn't realise how much I needed support too and I kept it all in.

Things got so bad that one night Simon had a meltdown with me.

We'd obviously not been getting along very well in the months beforehand and this particular night he arrived home from work once again at a very late hour – something that had been happening very frequently.

I was in bed when he eventually appeared and I probably made some sarcastic remark about the time.

To my surprise Simon blew up. 'That's it! I can't do this anymore. I'm leaving,' he said angrily. And with that he turned round, stormed out of the house, got in his car and drove away.

I was stunned.

It turned out he'd only gone to his parents' home and the next day he came back. I was relieved to see him. We needed to talk, that was obvious. The children, though not babies, were still at school and we didn't want to upset them. Plus, neither of us wanted our relationship to get worse, we wanted our marriage to work. We agreed we'd try to make more effort in the future.

****

My planned visit to the Arthur Findlay College was booked for early spring and I was quite excited as I threw an array of clothes into a large suitcase to take with me. What did they wear for these courses? I wondered. Comfortable casual, I decided but I added a couple of smarter bits too. Who knew what they did in the evenings at this place?

The college took a bit of finding but eventually I was cruising down a long drive through hedges and fields and turned a corner to see a huge, red brick, Jacobean style stately home spread out gracefully in front of me.

You'd never have believed you were only minutes from a busy airport. The mansion was surrounded by pristine lawns and gardens, huge old trees hugged the boundaries and somewhere round the back, a silvery lake glistened.

Later, I discovered this lovely building was called Stansted Hall and it had been bequeathed to the founders of the college by its Spiritualist owner, Arthur Findlay many years before. At the time though, my only thought was OMG – it's so overwhelming! What have I let myself in for?

I felt distinctly small and intimidated as I parked and dragged my bags up to the hefty oak door. Yet as I stepped nervously over the threshold I found myself in a snug, oak panelled reception area and a surprisingly warm, welcoming feeling washed over me. I immediately felt at home.

Two other women were checking in at the reception desk as I walked in and they turned and smiled.

'Hello,' said the dark-haired one, 'Have you been here before?'

'No, never,' I said.

'Well stick with us, we'll look after you!' they offered cheerfully.

And they did too. One of them was a care worker, the other a healer at the famous Harry Edwards healing sanctuary and just as their careers suggested, they were kindness itself. Friends for years, it turned out they were regular visitors to the college.

I checked in after them, then struggled up the ornate wooden staircase with my various bags to the bedrooms on the first floor. I was delighted to find my new friends had been put in the room next door. It was comforting to know they were only the other side of the wall. It was even more comforting to see that the toilet was only a few steps away up the corridor.

Good as their word, once we'd settled in they took me on a mini tour of the other ornate rooms where the various different classes were held. There was a green room and a blue room and all manner of other impressive chambers with high ceilings with intricate plasterwork, elaborate fireplaces and enormous mullioned windows overlooking the gardens. There was even a conservatory, known as the Sanctuary, a little gift shop and a huge oak-panelled, Persian-carpeted long gallery big enough to hold a ball in.

Yet most impressive of all were my fellow students. As everyone gathered in the bar before our introductory talk I was struck by the fact they all seemed to know each other and they were so friendly and kind. From all walks of life, a surprising number of them came from overseas. There were students from America, Australia, the Netherlands, Scandinavia – just about every corner of the globe – yet each obviously thought it worthwhile to travel thousands of miles to take a course at the Arthur Findlay College.

There was clearly nothing like it in their own countries. Some of them had come so far, I even felt a little guilty for having had to make so little effort myself – what was a few miles round the M25 compared to a long haul flight from Australia?

No one held it against me though and as I got to know this varied bunch, I realised that at last I'd found my tribe. These were my kind of people. No one seemed concerned about the car I drove, where I lived or whether my bag was designer or not. They didn't talk about private schools or where the next exotic holiday would be. Conversations here tended to flow around psychic subjects, things we'd experienced in the past and what we hoped to learn in the future. We were all on the same wavelength.

What's more everyone was a natural born empath – so if at any time you were feeling a little down, or worried or nervous, someone would immediately intuit your mood and do their best to cheer you up.

At last, possibly for the first time in my life, I felt really happy and comfortable in the company of a large group. The week flew past and yet it was like I'd been there forever. Our days were divided between attending lectures about the history and philosophy of Spiritualism, working with experienced mediums and healers and then practising our skills on each other.

It was a bit like being back at school – except my old teachers would have been stunned if they could have seen what an enthusiastic student I'd become. I turned up early for every lecture with my big notebook and pen, sat myself at the front of the class and took copious notes throughout each session.

I was like a sponge, eager for knowledge and couldn't get enough of the lessons.

Our meals were taken in the dining room and I later discovered that whatever table you sat at the first day you sat at for the whole week. During the evenings, we met up in the college bar and occasionally there were hilarious Karaoke nights.

By the end of the week I'd made dozens of new friends and like almost everyone else, I couldn't wait to go back. It was the most inspiring week of my life.

I even acquired a couple of affectionate nicknames. During one practice session a Scottish guy was so pleased with my reading for him he announced he was going to call me 'Doris' from now on, after the famous medium Doris Stokes.

One day waiting for a class to begin I found myself sitting next to my friend Peter. Suddenly the woman in front of him, a bright eyed young American named Dena, turned around and asked: 'Who is this? I don't know what it is but every time she speaks I see sparkles flying round in my head – so I'm gonna call you Sparkles,' she added to me.

As we chatted I admired the pretty heart-shaped diamante ring she was wearing. Instantly she took it off her finger and gave it to me.

'Oh no I couldn't!' I said, 'I didn't mean…'

'No that's fine,' she said, 'I have it for you. It's not valuable but I'd like you to have it.'

She was so insistent, I took it and Dena and I became good

friends. In fact to this day before starting a reading I put on that diamante ring.

Over the next few years I was to return many times to Stansted Hall and my skills as a medium and spiritual knowledge increased.

Sometimes I was startled by the unexpected things I saw. I was working with one fellow student late on a summer afternoon, when I saw an ancient Egyptian Princess with jewelled headdress, Kohl rimmed eyes and long robes, come and stand behind her. Quite a sight against the chintzy Victorian country house décor.

Open-mouthed I began describing this raven haired vision but my companion didn't seem particularly surprised.

'That's right,' she said, nodding cheerfully, 'I've been told before that my guide's an Egyptian princess. I'm glad she's here today.'

On other occasions, without warning the atmosphere would turn suddenly tragic. Once, partnered with a classmate from Holland, I found myself linking with a young girl who said she was my fellow student's sister. I was horrified to discover she'd committed suicide. It all got very emotional but the spirit sister wanted me to pass on the message that no one was to blame, she'd been very depressed over a failed relationship and a break up and that's what caused her to take such a desperate step.

My Dutch friend was wiping away the tears as I explained what I was hearing and I was worried I'd upset her, but she assured me it was ok. Every word was true and she was just delighted to have made contact with her sister at last.

Another time I was working with an unconventional student named David. David was probably the oldest gentleman there – being easily in his '80s. He was kind, but he could be very direct and plain-speaking at times. I was very fond of him and his sweetness made him a bit of a ladies' man, but he also had a knack of rubbing some people up the wrong way. So much so that whenever the group was asked to divide up into pairs – David tended to be the last to be picked.

When I realised what was happening I tried to step in before he noticed.

'I'll work with you David!' I used to tell him.

'Would you like to see the spirit world?' he asked rather surprisingly on one of these occasions, as we moved away from the group to start working.

'Of course,' I said wondering where this was leading.

'I can show you.'

'You can *show* me?' I couldn't quite work out what he meant but it had to be some sort of joke.

'Yes I can,' he said. 'Now shut your eyes…'

I shut my eyes.

'Now take a step,' said David.

I stepped forward, eyes still shut.

'Now take another step.'

I stepped again.

'Now stop and stand still,' said David, 'What do you see?'

Eyes still shut, I looked around in my mind's eye. I got a fleeting impression of a beautiful scene; peaceful green fields dotted with flowers spread out before me, the colours glowing in a way I'd never seen before and the whole landscape was flooded with light. Then, in a blink it was gone. I opened my eyes.

What *was* that?

David was beaming at me in delight. 'Did you see it?'

'Yes it was beautiful – just like I imagine Heaven,' I admitted. 'How did you *do* that?'

He just shrugged. I don't think he had any idea. Hard to believe it was a glimpse of the spirit world, but it was a glimpse of something. Anyway, we were meant to be working.

'Shall I start and see what I can get for you?' I asked, we'd found a quiet corner in the green room and sat down under one of the magnificent oil paintings.

David nodded. I got the feeling he enjoyed being at the college but wasn't particularly desperate to put in too much work himself. At his age who could blame him? He was desperately seeking something for himself and probably had no ambition to stand on a platform giving out messages.

I cleared my mind and started to focus. After a minute or two I was aware of a woman coming forward. She was a strong lady and she said her name was Jean and she was

David's wife.

'But there's someone else with her,' I went on. I could see a younger man beside her. He was many years younger than she was but they were arm in arm, obviously very close. In fact, it looked as if she was leading him round.

I asked David if he could place this couple because the younger man was obviously not her husband. 'Do you understand who they are? They're not a couple but they're close,' I said.

He said he did but he didn't elaborate.

I tried to speak to the younger man but he didn't want to say much. He just grinned and gestured towards the cap he was wearing. 'Andy Capp,' he told me, 'Andy Capp.' He gave me the impression of the comic character from the famous newspaper cartoon.

'I don't know if this means anything David,' I said, 'but it looks as if your wife is with someone. A younger man. He doesn't say much. He's wearing a cap and he's showing it to me and saying, 'Andy Capp. Andy Capp.' That's all and it looks as if your wife is taking him around. She's holding his arm.'

David's eyes filled with tears and he took my hand. 'Thank you,' he said, 'I've been coming for over 50 times, hoping for confirmation that our son has found his mother and proof they were together. This is the first time I've ever had it. I was so worried. He did often wear a cap but what I think he was trying to tell you is that he was handicapped. Our son was handicapped. That's why he couldn't speak. Andy Capp.'

Bev Mann

Andy Capp. How clever.

TEN:

What me stand on stage?
That wasn't going to happen ever...

Children grow up so fast don't they? One minute there I was cuddling my gorgeous little new born Rachel, so pretty with her pink ribbons and cute little matching outfits and now here she was, taller than me, a beautiful independent teenager, off to Warwick university.

Where did all the years go? I wondered as we set off in the car to look at student digs in Leamington Spa, a pretty town, convenient for the university. Student accommodation was in such demand we had to move fast and dash up the motorway to sign tenancy agreements months before the term started.

Unfortunately, Rachel's flat mate wasn't able to come with us that day but she trusted Rachel to make the right choice for them both. So what could possibly go wrong? Well for a start, when we pulled up outside the address the estate agent had given us I began to feel apprehensive. The converted Victorian house looked shabby and unloved and as we climbed the rickety stairs to the student rooms at the top, the depressing air only got worse.

Hearts sinking, we opened the door to the flat and immediately a sharp smell of damp hit us in the face, then quickly grabbed us by the throats. The rooms were tiny and extravagant sprays of dark green mould marched across every wall. As for the bathroom, it was enough to make you feel sick.

Poor Rachel had been so hoping the place would be nice, but her face fell.

'You can't stay here Rachel,' I said, 'You'll be ill.'

'Oh Mum,' said Rachel. She hated a fuss but I could tell she didn't like it either.

'Come on, let's take the key back to the estate agent and see if there's anywhere else.'

'There won't be Mum,' said Rachel, 'Everything's already gone.'

But there was no way we could sign a tenancy agreement for this unsanitary place. Back we went to the car and retraced the route to the estate agent's.

Unsurprisingly, the letting part of the office was very busy as we walked in and I could see the young woman dealing with the queue was getting a little stressed. No doubt she was having to disappoint a lot of frustrated customers that day.

When it was our turn I quickly explained the situation. 'So you see my daughter can't stay there. In fact nobody should stay there, it's a health hazard,' I said, handing back the key. 'That mould will make anyone ill. Have you got anything else that might be suitable?'

The young lady shook her head. 'I'm sorry Mrs Mann, this is our busiest time. There's nothing left.'

But as she was speaking I found my eyes drawn to her desk. Next to the piles of papers and the phone I could see what was plainly a set of angel cards, half hidden by a notebook.

She saw me looking at them. 'My cards,' she said, 'Are you interested in that sort of thing?'

'Yes, I am!' I said, 'It's what I do. I'm a medium.'

'Really!' she looked pleased. 'I'll pick a card for you shall I?'

'No it's ok,' I said, 'Let me do something for you.' And hardly had I finished speaking when I noticed a smiling elderly woman step forward to stand next to the letting agent. She beamed fondly at the young woman then showed me that she was holding a baby in her arms.

'There's a lady here,' I said to the agent, 'I feel it's your grandmother. She's holding a baby and looking at you with such love. I have a feeling the baby belongs to you.'

The letting agent sat down suddenly, her face pale, eyes filling with tears. 'That's right,' she whispered, 'I lost a baby. I had a miscarriage.'

I could have kicked myself. I shouldn't have blurted that out.

'I'm so sorry,' I apologised.

But the woman wasn't embarrassed at all. 'No, no don't be sorry. Thank you. That means such a lot, to know the baby's there, with my nan.'

The news seemed to have made her day. She was really happy to hear her baby was safe and being taken care of by her much loved grandmother. The grandmother left her with some reassuring words and hope for the future.

With that, the girl got up and hugged me. I looked round to see Rachel squirming with embarrassment, mixed with secret admiration. I realised she'd never seen me in action before.

'I'm really sorry we've got no other flats at the moment,' the agent went on, as she walked us to the door, 'It's been so nice to meet you. This is such a busy time but if anything else comes in, I'll let you know straight away.'

It was the best we could do. There was no option but to turn round and go home. So off we went, back down the motorway, with no flat for Rachel and a wasted journey. At least we'd managed to avoid a health hazard I told myself, trying to think positive, and maybe we'd been sent to give a much needed message to that young woman. Yes, maybe that was the point of the trip.

A couple of hours later we finally rolled back into our Hertfordshire street. I pulled into the drive, turned off the engine and picked up my phone. Annoying! I'd just missed a call.

Strange. It was the estate agent's number. I looked at my watch. It was three minutes to 6pm. There was just about time to call back. Had we left something behind in the office?

'You'll never believe this Mrs Mann,' she said, 'but a cancellation for a new, purpose-built student flat has just this minute come in. This is very unusual. Are you interested?'

Were we interested?!!!

The upshot was, a few days later Rachel and had secured the

ideal accommodation for the coming year.

'You know, this medium business - it comes in handy now and then doesn't it?' I said to Rachel tongue in cheek.

Rachel gave a little smile. High praise indeed from a teenager.

In truth this 'medium business' was getting better and better. I'd learned a lot at the college and though I went back frequently for additional residential courses on different aspects of the work, I was still shy but slowly gaining confidence. I had been giving low-key, one to one readings for friends and their friends also helped out at charity events and school fetes.

I was still nervous of standing on a platform and working in front of an audience. Whenever I was on a course that involved a little platform practice, I tended to run for the door. The tutors were usually understanding and invariably allowed me and others who felt the same to go out to the long gallery and work one to one with each other.

I never had an ambition to be a platform medium. Me stand on stage? With rows of people staring at me? You had to be joking. That wasn't going to happen. Ever! I said to myself. It was like my worst nightmare. Yet after a while, watching so many of my classmates bravely agreeing to give it a go, I felt I was being a bit cowardly to avoid the practise every time. After all, here amongst my fellow students and tutors it wasn't like performing in the outside world. Here I'd be as safe as I could possibly be. Maybe I should at least try it to gain a little experience. So one day, instead of running for the door, I forced myself to stay put with the other budding platform workers.

When my turn came to walk to the top of the room, the old familiar fear of reading in front of the class swept over me. My head was whirling but I made my feet ascend the two or three steps to the platform and found myself suddenly looking out over the assorted heads.

My heart was racing, mouth dry but by using my breath to calm my mind, I managed to concentrate, tune in to a higher vibration, to deliver a message. It was a man - a bus conductor called Ernie he told me. He was wearing a dark uniform and he showed me one of those old fashioned ticket machines that you wound with a handle. It reminded me of the old TV comedy On the Buses and I felt that this man was just like the main character, Sam Butler. Fortunately, someone in the audience recognised Ernie as their uncle. I was so glad because now we were introduced I got quite fond of Ernie. He made me feel at ease.

He told me lots of the funny little expressions he used to use in life, which made his niece laugh and my whole practice passed in a very amusing, light-hearted way. When we finished, I slid gratefully back down the steps to resume my seat. Wow. My turn had come and gone for the day and I'd survived!

The following day full of nervous excitement as my first attempt had gone so well I decided to give it another try. Only this time round the tutor wasn't overly encouraging. The information I'd given was ok it seemed but: 'Trouble is, you're a bit boring to watch Bev,' she said. 'You just stand there – stock still, which is dull for the audience. Notice how the other mediums move about the platform when they're talking? You should try to be a bit more mobile.'

Bit more mobile? I was so rigid with fright up there in front of people it was all I could do to stand up, let alone get my legs to work.

Fortunately, as the years went on, it got easier. I began to relax a little more, the knots in my stomach weren't quite so tight, my palms not so sweaty. Yet it was still torture on some occasions. Late one afternoon when we were all tired from a long day, the new tutor who was just starting her first week, asked me to get up on the platform.

I was reluctant, knowing how tired I was but felt I should make an effort for spirit. Unfortunately, I got completely stuck with a spirit contact who wanted to communicate. It was a woman and she kept showing me, playing cards, casino tables and roulette wheels. I have to say I couldn't make head nor tail of what she was trying to tell me. Worse – neither could anyone else. No one in the audience could place her.

The woman kept on fiddling about with her roulette wheel, spinning it around and holding up various pieces in no particular order, but otherwise couldn't seem to make herself clear. It didn't help. My descriptions of what I was seeing were met with silence and blank eyes. I began to feel quite desperate and wish I hadn't stood up.

After what seemed like hours but was probably only a few minutes, the tutor stepped in to help. She tuned in herself and managed to link in with the same lady.

'Yes you've definitely got a spirit person,' she said, 'but I think she had dementia, that's why some of the information coming through is a bit weird. She's presenting as she was, before she passed – confused.'

At that, several people in the audience put up their hands. The reference to dementia had obviously rung a bell for them. Perhaps whichever one of them turned out to be related to the poor lady, hadn't known she entertained herself in her last years playing cards. I'm not sure now which member of the audience was finally identified as the relative, but at least, after that embarrassing interlude, we'd established the contact. Everyone seemed satisfied – except me. I was upset at the whole experience.

Yet as I stepped off the platform at the end I heard one of the international students say to the tutor: 'Do you think Bev could have been fabricating that?'

I was horrified. It had been so difficult and such an effort. How could she think I was making it up? Why would I do that?

Thankfully not all my platform experiences were so tricky.

Once, the wonderful, renowned medium and teacher Glyn Edwards, now sadly passed away, was taking the class in the Sanctuary. When it was my turn, I climbed up on the platform in my usual, slightly reluctant way but it wasn't long before the information was flowing and I moved from link to link.

Then after a while, a new presence came forward. I got the impression of an exotic Indian woman. She was showing me a beautiful pond covered in water lilies. Then she showed me people lighting candles, putting them inside the water lilies and letting them float. I was staring down at dozens and dozens of tiny flames glowing across the pond. It was magical. I also got the word Swarmi.'

I looked out over the audience. Who's going to take this one I thought. No one said anything. No hand went up. Hopeless, I was thinking again, my heart beginning to sink, I so wanted things to go well with Glyn watching.

Then an amazing thing happened. Out of the corner of my eye I saw Glyn himself nodding approvingly.

'I can accept her,' he said, 'I know who she is. She's a past teacher and friend of mine.'

Thrilled, I was able to pass on more messages from the lady to Glyn and he seemed very impressed.

When I'd finished we broke for lunch but afterwards, on the way back to class I bumped into Glyn coming in from the garden.

'I've got a little present for you,' he said mysteriously, and he handed me a tiny package wrapped in tissue paper.

Puzzled, I carefully prised open the tissue and found myself looking at a single, green leaf, freshly picked.

'Eh, thank you Glyn,' I said uncertainly.

'That's a leaf from Gordon Higginson's favourite tree,' Glyn explained.

Gordon Higginson was a famous medium of the 20th century and for many years the greatly revered President of the

Spiritualist National Union which owned the college. He was credited with sorting out the college's finances and steering the institution to success. These days his portrait hung in a prominent position in the library and though he passed away in 1993, you got the feeling he was still keeping an eye on the place and you could sense his presence.

'This is my gift to you,' Glyn went on indicating the leaf, 'Don't ever change your mediumship. Don't ever change for anyone.'

Glyn was one of the few tutors left at the college who'd actually known Gordon well by all accounts, so perhaps that's why the great man often seemed to be close when Glyn was around.

I was reminded of this on another occasion when I'd had a difficult day. I went into the garden during the break and sat on the bench staring at Gordon's Tulip tree. 'Am I even supposed to be doing this?' I said out loud in frustration. I need a sign I'm on the right path. There was no answer. Nothing changed. I hadn't really expected it to. After a while I calmed down and went back inside.

The good thing was that the next session after lunch was with Glyn. His classes always cheered me up, they were so inspiring. This time he asked us students to get into pairs and take it in turns to do readings for each other, while Glyn moved around us, observing and helping out where necessary.

When it was my partner's turn to read for me, she went very quiet as she focused to find a link. The minutes ticked by, then she got something: 'I've got a male presence here,' she said, 'he's a big man, with grey hair. He feels powerful and knowledgeable… he could even be some sort of spiritual teacher… he's showing me… an apple.'

An apple? I was always hoping for a contact with my dad but I couldn't place what he might mean by an apple.

'And he's saying – you already have it. Own it. Be your own individuality – the core of yourself.'

Ah 'core' I thought. That must explain the apple. Very symbolic but it doesn't sound like dad.

'He says he can see you're on the right path,' my partner went on, 'He sees you've got it. He wants you to be sure to uphold all the values of the Spiritualist family; integrity, passion, love, patience, interest – always growing. Always learning. You have his blessing…'

I was amazed, it sounded like the kind of thing Gordon Higginson would say, 'Well who is he?' I asked.

My partner listened intently. 'She said I don't feel this man is your father… He's showing me a gold signet ring with engraving on it.'

Could we possibly be talking to the actual Gordon Higginson?

I looked round at Glyn who was moving from pair to pair, helping or making comments to each student.

'Glyn!' I said, 'Could you check this out for us?' And as he came over I whispered, as I didn't want my partner to freak out. 'I think we might have got Gordon Higginson over here.'

Intrigued, Glyn came over and stood beside my partner. He closed his eyes for a moment, to tune in, then he smiled.

'Yes,' he said, 'Well done both of you. You've had the privilege of a message from Gordon himself. Write it down Bev so you don't forget his words.'

Fortunately, I'd been taking notes so I already had the precious message to keep. My partner felt really honoured to be Gordon's chosen medium and I was thrilled I'd had answer to my garden plea for a sign. We both wandered around in a bit of a daze for the rest of the afternoon!

So my mediumship was progressing nicely but the same couldn't be said of other aspects of my life.

I realise now the trouble was, as far as my old life was concerned, I was changing. Developing as a medium was actually turning me into a different person.

These days I try to warn my students of this strange effect because as your eyes are opened to a different perspective, the other people in your life who haven't shared your experiences may no longer 'gel' with you the way they did before. It can lead to all sorts of unintended consequences.

Suddenly you're meeting all sorts of new people, people from all walks of life and from all over the world, people with different ideas, different ways of viewing things. Your mind expands, your horizons expand and it's wonderful – but it can be hard to accept for some of your old friends who can scarcely recognise you any more.

It certainly didn't improve my relationship with Simon. A few years before, there'd come a very low point in our marriage when completely out of the blue I got an anonymous poison phone call on my mobile when I was out with a friend. An unfamiliar male voice said: 'Is that Beverley Mann? You need to watch your husband with a certain woman. They're spending a lot of time together.' And he named her.

This person, was even someone close that I knew. Someone I considered to be a family friend. Then he put the phone down.

I was chilled to the bone. The receiver slipped out of my hand. Suddenly I felt sick and dizzy. My world was crashing down and I could hardly contain myself. I called Simon at his office and told him what had happened. He denied it but said he'd come home immediately as I was upset. While I was waiting I phoned the woman but she also said it was totally untrue.

And of course when Simon arrived he reassured me again. He was working so hard and doing so well perhaps it's not surprising some jealous rival might want to spoil things for him.

With the children settled and at school, the house comfortable and homely it seemed crazy to worry about a malicious rumour. Yet it was a nasty experience. To think, that man had my phone number and was quite intentionally wanting to cause us trouble, to spoil our relationship. It made me feel quite ill to imagine. What must have been going through his mind to say such a thing?

And yet, the more I thought about it, the more I could see that despite enjoying some lovely holidays together little by little, we were still developing in different directions – and the pace was accelerating. We realised that we needed some outside help to get our marriage back on track. We decided to go for counselling. But I didn't realise till much later that we were only papering over the cracks.

Mum's poor health didn't help either. The cold and the damp made her bad back worse so as we were lucky enough to have a flat in Spain, I was able to whisk her and the kids off to the sunshine as often as I could.

While I was getting more and more involved in my psychic pursuits, Simon had taken up cycling, quite seriously. He threw himself into gruelling charity bike rides which of course required long training sessions and weeks away with his cycling mates. He loved it and the exercise worked wonders for his fitness but sadly, it was yet another passion we didn't share.

The situation had been evolving so gradually I hadn't realised quite how difficult my life had become until my 50th birthday loomed and suddenly I was shocked to realise I was being split in two.

It started harmlessly enough. We decided to throw a massive party to celebrate my half century.

I love fancy dress. 'Everyone can come as a character whose name begins with 'B'!' I said.

It was a lovely thought and at first I was thrilled with the idea. The old Bev adored dressing up and having fun. Well, the new Bev does as well, I have to admit, but in a different way.

Anyway there we were, knee deep in plans for a marquee in the garden, cheeky butlers in the buff and recipes for exotic cocktails, when Mum had a fall from the car and injured her back and ribs and was in hospital. Suddenly a party didn't seem like such a good idea. But Simon said it was too late to cancel.

I became more and more anxious. Then my eye fell on the ever expanding guest list. As I glanced down the names it suddenly struck me that they fell into two very distinct categories. There were our old friends and acquaintances and various business associates of Simon's – quite a large contingent of 'plastics' amongst them, then there were my new friends from the local development circles plus the cosmopolitan crowd from college.

A nasty little knot of anxiety began to creep into my stomach. How was that going to work, I wondered? One lot talking the latest creations from Prada while the others discussed the pros and cons of trance mediumship?

I suspected they wouldn't get on and each camp would be wondering how the Bev they knew, could possibly fit into the other group.

I looked again at Simon's lavish plans. Our old set would expect nothing less but what would my new friends make of it? They were an unmaterialistic bunch. Would they think I was trying to be too posh, or too flash?

It may sound silly now, but the dilemma began to worry me more and more. As the big day approached I worked myself up into quite a state. I could hardly eat, I felt jumpy and nervous all the time. It was crazy. This was supposed to be a celebration. I was doing this for fun yet what with my mum in hospital as well, in my head it was turning into a nightmare. Maybe we should call it off I thought again. But then everything was booked, the invitations had gone out, our guests would be disappointed and some were even flying in from abroad. Simon couldn't understand why I was so bothered.

Well as it turned out, despite my worries, the party was a big success. Simon went as a Beatle from the Sergeant Pepper era in a colourful, military inspired suit, then an old boyfriend dressed as a Beatle from the earlier mop top era turned up, so the two of them had a good laugh. As I'd lost so much weight with worry, I'd suddenly realised there was a silver lining. I could get away with going as a Burlesque dancer in a skimpy costume, showing off my newly slender waist! I hadn't always been slim so it was good to make the most of it.

And to my relief, it seemed as if the guests were enjoying themselves. The marquee looked amazing, the drinks were flowing, the almost naked butlers were a big hit and with a few of those exotic cocktails I began to relax. I can't say I didn't have a good time. I did. Yet despite the fun, the event crystallised my feelings. As I wandered round the garden I couldn't fail to notice the party had divided into two markedly separate groups. The old set and my new friends. While they didn't exactly clash – they didn't mix either.

Then as the evening wore on, I was chatting to one of the

plastics when an Arthur Findlay student walked by – dressed as a biker, resplendent in faded jeans and a tee shirt that showed off his extravagant American Indian tattoos.

Our plastic guest stared at him in admiration. 'Where did you buy those fake tatts?' she asked. 'They're so cool.'

My student friend blinked, a bit amazed. His striking, intricate and highly detailed tattoos had taken a lot of time and effort. He couldn't quite believe anyone would mistake them for fakes. Was she joking? No she wasn't.

'Oh… no they're not fake,' he said kindly, when he realised she was serious. 'I got them done in Canada - by the native Indians.'

The next day when he phoned to thank us for a lovely day, he reminded me of the incident. 'Great party Bev, but what planet are your friends on?'

I had to laugh with him but that's when the truth I'd been avoiding for so long, hit me. The two sides of my life were in separate compartments but it was getting increasingly difficult to keep them that way. I couldn't go on like this - trying to keep one foot in each world. In the end I had to make a choice. I needed to go where I really belonged.

ELEVEN:

'Your feet aren't going to touch the ground…' he said.

I seemed to spend a lot of my time feeling confused at this point, yet whenever I found myself cruising down the long driveway towards the welcoming lawns and red-brick splendour of the Arthur Findlay College for a further course, the problems of the outside world faded away and it was like I was coming home.

It was a welcome break from my actual home, where those niggles of doubt about my marriage were getting stronger and stronger. My psychic studies and new friends were occupying more and more of my mind and my time, while Simon's work and his sport events were having the same effect on him. Sometimes it seemed as if we only saw each other in passing and when we did go out together to some function, I still couldn't quite get over those same old feelings of inferiority the smart set still inspired in me.

Against this backdrop, my visits to the college came as a huge relief. The rigours of the coursework distracted me from thinking about anything else. There was always an element of excitement too about starting a new course. I soon noticed a funny thing. You could never tell where the next course might lead you. Each visit seemed to spark me off in different and quite unexpected directions.

During a course you often got the chance to have an individual assessment of your development with one of the tutors – this was known as spiritual assessment. But this was no ordinary teacher's opinion of a student's work in class. No, the tutor was there to channel spirits for *their* advice and comments on how you were doing.

This was always quite exciting as you could never guess what they were going to say and they quite often took you by surprise.

At one of my early sessions the lady tutor and I were sitting in one of the college's smaller, cosy rooms where these private meetings took place, when she suddenly made contact with an American Indian guide.

I don't know what I was expecting, but it certainly wasn't what he said.

'He's telling me that you're a great teacher,' the tutor explained. 'You should start teaching. Right now!'

The idea seemed so crazy, I laughed. For a start I felt I still had a lot to learn myself so the idea of me teaching others seemed completely wrong. And second – I still had my phobia of standing up in front of people, addressing them. Put those two obstacles together and the idea of taking up teaching was a non-starter.

'Well I'm sorry,' said the tutor, when I explained it was impossible, 'but they're quite firm about it. They want you to teach. You don't have to do anything too dramatic to start with. Create your own circle. Begin with just a few people – six, say – and take it from there.'

I had severe doubts of course. It wasn't something I wanted to do, and the idea had never entered my head as I arrived at the college a few days earlier. Yet by the time I drove away, the feeling I must give teaching a try was overwhelming.

Back home I dutifully put the word around that I was thinking of starting a small circle. If the spirit world wanted me to do it, they would find the people. And sure enough twelve accepted my invitation. On the agreed evening I made a space in our quiet basement room, with the now perfectly behaved cupboard. I arranged comfortable chairs around a table and put out a jug of water and some glasses.

Then suddenly the door-bell rang and all twelve eager students were pouring into the hall, all keen to hear what I had to say.

I was nervous but delighted as I led them downstairs. But as I settled them round the table it began to dawn on me that on my visits to the college, I wasn't just learning the subjects on the particular course I'd chosen, I was also observing how the tutors worked with the class and without even realising it, absorbing how to teach.

Each tutor had their own special way of communicating with the students, I noticed. They each had their different, distinctive styles and methods, and some resonated with me better than others. Unconsciously I'd been storing it all away and now, confronted with my own 'students', I was able to bring out the sort of approaches that had helped me most, blended with my own personality.

It seemed to work. By the end of the evening I had a circle.

My students actually wanted to come back the following week and amazingly I'd ended up enjoying the session myself. I felt elated. It was incredible! So now, as well as being a medium, I was also a teacher! How did that happen?

And all because I'd attended that course at the college on a different subject entirely.

On another visit I found myself having an assessment with the kindly Glyn Edwards.

'My! You're going to be so busy,' he said when we got started, 'Your feet aren't going to touch the ground. You'll be working here and abroad and you'll be living out of a suitcase.'

He stopped and glanced over his shoulder, 'Oh, now Gordon Higginson's come in. He's walking up and down. He's telling me that that's right. You're going to be very busy. You're one of the troupers!'

I was thrilled of course but couldn't quite see how it was all going to happen.

Yet not long afterwards I bumped into a fellow student – an American woman called Carrie.

'Every time you walk by, I notice the lovely scent you're wearing. You smell so good!' she said, 'What is it?'

'It's called Romance,' I said, flattered, 'by Ralph Lauren. I've worn it for years. I love it.'

'It's gorgeous,' said Carrie, 'I must look out for some when I get home!'

Well Carrie and I ended up becoming great friends after that and before she left, she invited me over to visit her in Boston for a holiday.

We kept in touch and a few months later, when I had time for a break, I took up her offer. I love the USA and it was wonderful to get the chance to be shown round Boston by someone who really knew the city.

Carrie met me off the bus from the airport and we began a whirlwind tour of the sites. I particularly enjoyed Quincy's Market – an historic building with a Doric column façade like a Greek temple and a beautiful central dome, the whole place buzzing with interesting stalls and eateries.

What really surprised me though was the snow! It was late winter and the streets were lined with icy, grey mountains of slush, shovelled up from the roads, which then froze solid where it was piled. In the UK I was used to our small flurries of the white stuff that caused brief havoc for a day or two then quickly thawed, but here the remnants stood 10ft tall! Plus of course I wasn't wearing the right shoes and slipped and slid all over the place!

Despite the cold I had a great time. Boston is a wonderful city. As it turned out Carrie had her own private spiritual practice above a shop in town and she took me along to see it. It was fascinating. I met some of her clients and before I left I even conducted my own workshop there. Carrie's clients were interested to see the English way of doing these things but nevertheless, Carrie was keen to give me a big build up.

'We've got to think of the right way to describe what you do,' she mused. 'I know – Mediumship from the Heart! I just got that from Spirit. It's perfect.'

I thought it sounded ideal. In fact, I liked it so much I've been using it ever since. 'Mediumship from the Heart' seemed to sum up exactly what I was trying to do.

The workshop went very well with 22 eager students, and I thoroughly enjoyed meeting Carrie's Boston friends. But that was just the beginning of my association with this little corner of the USA. Next thing I knew I was invited back to take a service at the first Spiritualist church of Salem – the town famous the world over for its controversial 17th century witch trials – but now a pretty seaside resort, only half an hour by road from Boston.

This time I opted to visit in the summer and hired a car too. I was so glad I did. Salem turned out to be the loveliest place. I found myself wandering through shady, tree-lined streets dotted with historic clap-board houses. There was a bustling harbour and waterfront and everywhere I looked I noticed witchy reminders of the town's past. There was a witch museum, witch themed tea-rooms and coffee shops, taxi-cabs decked out with little witch logos and there was even a statue of Elizabeth Montgomery, the actress who starred in Bewitched – my childhood heroine! There were also some lovely shops with crystals and spiritual trinkets.

I'd never been to Salem before, yet as I drove through the quaint streets I got the strangest feelings of déjà vu. I felt completely at home – even more so when I noticed a signpost for the town of Beverly – just up the coast!

The First Salem Spiritualist Church turned out to be an attractive, turn of the last century building that started life as a Quaker Meeting house. Set back from the road in another graceful, tree-lined residential area, it had a set of wooden steps leading up to the picturesque front porch and inside in the main body of the church was a stained glass window featuring the star of David. The sight of that traditional Jewish symbol put me at ease straight away! Just as well, or I might have been even more daunted when I walked in to find around 80 people waiting expectantly to hear what I had to say. More and more people kept arriving and the organisers had to find more chairs. Eek!

Mouth as dry as toast, I joined the traditional procession - consisting of the pastor and another officer of the church - to walk up the aisle and climb onto the podium at the front. As usual I had to fight to control my nerves but thank Heavens my guides didn't let me down. But then of course I know really that they never let us down, and soon the messages were flowing.

One of them stuck in my memory particularly. A male voice came forward in my mind. He'd committed suicide he explained and he wanted to speak to his wife's aunt who was sitting a few rows back. He just wanted to tell her he was sorry for all the trouble he'd caused he said. It turned out he'd been leading a double life, shuttling between his wife and a mistress – neither of whom knew about the other. It was all beginning to get too complicated for him and he wasn't happy. And then came the bombshell that pushed him over the edge. Both women fell pregnant at the same time. The poor man didn't know how to cope – so in a fit of panic, he killed himself.

It was a sad story but I think his wife's aunt was glad to hear his apology and know that he was genuinely sorry. She promised to pass this news on to his wife.

Another memorable contact came from a man who'd lost his life in the terrible Twin Towers terrorist attack. He'd been high up in one of the offices when the buildings were struck and he didn't stand a chance. Unfortunately, none of his relatives were in the congregation that day but a family friend happened to be there. So he asked this lady if she would pass on the message that he was absolutely fine now, and they must stop worrying about what he went through. He was ok and often came to see what they were up to. He was still part of their family even though they couldn't see him.

But maybe the most surprising moment came a few days later, when one of the church officials asked if I could do a private reading for her friend. She showed us to the secretary's office and we sat beside the desk.

I was immediately linked with this lady's partner and she seemed very happy with the evidence and messages. Then, towards the end of the reading a different voice came in.

'I've got an older gentleman here,' I said, 'Who seems to be a teacher of some kind. I think he taught you.'

The woman nodded expectantly.

'And… and I'm inspired to give you this picture.' This was very puzzling. For quite a while now I'd been in the habit of carrying a photo of Gordon Higginson around with me in my handbag – for inspiration and moral support. Nobody knew that, but now this spirit person was asking me to get out the photo and give it to the lady in front of me.

Baffled I picked up my bag and found the photo.

'Here we are,' I said taking it out, 'I don't know why, but he wants me to give you this.'

I handed the picture over and the woman's mouth fell open.

'That's Gordon Higginson,' she said.

'Yes, it is,' I agreed, surprised. 'You recognise him?'

'Of course!' she said, 'Years ago I took a course at the Arthur Findlay College in England and Gordon Higginson was my teacher! I'll never forget him.'

For once, I was speechless.

After that first visit I returned to Salem many times. I loved the town so much, especially the shopping. I often went back for holidays. In fact, I even toyed with the idea of moving there permanently. One spring I was visiting again, with the vague idea of checking out the houses for sale and as usual I emailed ahead to my friend Pat who ran the Spiritualist church.

'Hi Pat,' I wrote, 'I'm going to be in Salem on May 9th – would you like me to be the medium at the church that day?'

Pat checked the church diary. 'Oh, what a shame,' she wrote back, 'We've already got a medium for the 9th. But thanks for thinking of us. Let me know a bit further in advance next time – we'd love to have you back.'

Salem in the spring was even prettier than ever so I had a good time revisiting my favourite haunts and on May 9th I decided to pop into the Spiritualist church to say 'hello' to Pat and my other friends and attend the service.

As I walked up the familiar steps Pat was just coming out. She gave me a friendly wave but oddly, she didn't look surprised to see me, even though I hadn't mentioned I'd be coming.

Then she looked me up and down and her face fell a little. 'You're kidding me!' she said gesturing to my clothes.

I looked down at my outfit. It wasn't that bad, surely? Just my usual comfortable holiday gear – jeans and a summery top and trainers.

'You've brought something to change into, right?' said Pat.

'Change into?' I echoed, puzzled. 'No…'

'But you're not thinking of going on the podium like that, surely?' Pat looked quite worried now.

'The podium?' I was even more puzzled now, 'No I'm in the congregation. I thought this outfit would be fine…I'll sit at the back if you like.'

Now Pat looked puzzled. 'Didn't you get my message?'

It turned out the medium booked for the 9th had cancelled at the last minute and Pat had left a message on my phone asking me to take the service after all.

'OMG – I didn't get it!' I shrieked. 'It's pure chance I came over here today. Give me half an hour. I'll dash back to the hotel and change.' Because I knew that at Salem Church they liked to do things properly. The medium ought at least to wear something a bit smarter than jeans, out of respect for the spirit world.

Fortunately, everything went well after that. 'You see Pat,' I said when the service finished, 'I knew I was meant to be the medium on May 9th!'

All in all, just as Glyn Edwards predicted, I spent a lot of time living out of a suitcase in the years following his assessment.

Time went on and the readings and the teaching were going well. Invitations were flowing in from all over the place and I was beginning to think my psychic life at least, was shaping up well. Then, just as I was getting into my stride, I hit another unexpected but painfully difficult patch.

It started innocuously enough. I so enjoyed my teaching I began to wonder if there was any way I could eventually become a tutor at the college.

I so loved the place it would be like a dream come true I decided. And it wasn't as impossible as you might think because there was a series of exams you could take to gain the necessary Spiritualist National Union qualifications to become a tutor. It might take a while to cover all the required elements but at least it was a well laid path to my goal.

I made a start with the best of intentions. I had to study and produce a number of essays by a set date. Nothing wrong with that of course and I fully intended to meet the deadline. But then my poor old mum was taken ill again.

Her condition must have crept up on us little by little. We noticed occasionally that she didn't look as well as usual, but we can all vary from day to day can't we? So we didn't think much of it. Then one afternoon I'd popped over for a chat and was horrified to notice she looked quite yellow. She insisted she felt fine. But her face had a decidedly mustard tint and even the whites of her eyes were no longer white. She looked as if she had a bad case of jaundice.

Lorraine and I insisted she get checked out by the doctor. As is the way of these things, the doctor was concerned and sent her for further tests. There were a lot of appointments and hospital visits to take her to and after much to-ing and fro-ing we were eventually told she had cancer. Once again, just like before with my dad, I found myself listening to a consultant coming out with the dreadful prognosis: 'I'm very sorry Mrs Mann. There's nothing we can do. No suitable treatment. I'm afraid your mother doesn't have long to live – a few months at the most.'

It was devastating. The awful memories of my father's last days came flooding back and a bewildering grief flowed over me again – past grief for my father mixed with new grief for my mother. Yet these gut-wrenching feelings had to be hidden away whenever Mum was around. If she didn't have long left, I was determined she should enjoy every day as much as was humanly possible and Mum felt the same way.

In fact, after a small procedure to stop the jaundice, Mum really didn't feel too bad. So, as she appeared well enough to travel, I started arranging what we assumed would be her last holiday, a family trip to Tenerife for Christmas and the New

Year.

Underneath, I was distraught. Mum and I were very close and even though she was in her late '80s I wasn't ready to part with her yet. I was torn in two trying to put on a cheerful smile when we were together to keep her happy, but smile and chatter I did, and Mum tried to carry on much as usual.

Unfortunately, a side effect of this emotional roller-coaster was an inability to get on with writing my essays. Every time I sat down to put a few words on paper, my mind would wander and I'd start thinking about Mum.

The deadline was getting closer and closer which only added to my worries. The more panicked I became about the amount of work to do, the less I produced. In the end I contacted the SNU. I explained the situation about my gravely ill Mum and asked if I could have more time for my essays. They agreed, but sadly the most they said they could allow was two weeks – which given the amount still to cover and the time I needed to care for Mum, was impossible.

There was no alternative. I'd have to put my dreams of becoming a tutor on hold. Then another unexpected blow fell. During this traumatic time over the Christmas holiday, I'd been keeping in touch with the other students online on our special student Facebook page. Somehow I got into a disagreement with one of the tutors who happened to be on there. We exchanged a few terse comments but that was all and I thought no more about it.

Then a curious thing happened. For some time, I'd been a member of the Spiritualist National Union but with all the dramas over Mum I'd completely forgotten to renew my membership on the due date.

When I got back from Tenerife the accounts department got in touch to remind me that I still needed to pay. Yet something made me hold back. 'Don't do it,' a spirit voice at the back of my mind whispered. So I delayed, held onto my subscription and let the matter lie.

I thought nothing of it at the time, but a few weeks later, the reason for the advised delay became clear. Out of the blue, I received a letter and accompanying summons from the SNU which runs the college, to say that a formal complaint had been made against me. I was being summoned to attend proceedings of arbitration. The tribunal would investigate my alleged 'offence' of defamation.

I was absolutely horrified – and frightened too. I immediately imagined having to present myself at some sort of courtroom and being made to stand in the dock being cross-examined by a stony faced panel.

Would it really have been like that? I don't know, but just the thought of it made my legs go so weak I had to fall into a chair.

How could a few off-the-cuff exchanges online have led to this? My beloved college was so important to me it was like the bottom had fallen out of my world. Upset and quite desperate, I confided in a college friend. She pointed out that as my membership had lapsed, they couldn't take me to a tribunal anyway as I was no longer a member of the Union.

Despite this I wrote a nine-page letter to the SNU explaining again that my mum was dying and assuring them I'd assumed the exchange was no more than a simple misunderstanding. And besides, since I was no longer a member of the Union, they couldn't summon me to appear before them.

I didn't get a response to my comments.

Instead a formal letter arrived. There was no mention of my mother or my difficulties, just a clipped statement that since I was no longer a member of the SNU my appearance before the tribunal had been cancelled.

I was massively relieved, but also hurt that a spiritual organisation couldn't have been more understanding.

TWELVE:
The woman said, 'I want to stick pins in my husband's eyes...'

I was walking down the corridor towards Mum's flat when it happened. Mum had sold the Edgware house long ago and these days lived in a comfortable apartment in a retirement block. As the hospital could do nothing more for her, she was back home now, determined to carry on as normal and so today, in typical Mum-fashion, she'd invited her three best friends over for tea.

I'd popped in to say hello and see if the elderly ladies needed anything. Yet as I headed towards Mum's front door, sad as ever about the hopelessness of her condition, a spirit voice stopped me in my tracks.

'It's not her time,' it said.

'What?' I thought. The consultant had been so sure. There had been so many tests – the results all depressing. The doctors were quite certain Mum had only a few months left, at most. So how could it possibly not be her time?

And yet: 'It's not her time to come over,' the voice repeated insistently, 'In fact she will not be the first of that group to pass.'

This sounded unlikely too. As far as I knew, though all three of Mum's friends were aged over 80, none of them was unwell, while Mum had terminal cancer. So how could the voice be right?

Yet I knew by now to trust these unseen messengers. I don't think they'd ever been wrong. So, impossible as the prediction sounded, it must be true. A spark of hope shot through me and instantly my mood soared. I practically danced down the rest of the corridor. Somehow, I had no idea how, Mum was going to live!

I breezed through the tea party with a big smile on my face, but I couldn't tell anyone why I was suddenly so happy. They'd think I was crazy. It was a secret I had to keep to myself.

Back home afterwards, I bustled about preparing a meal, hungrier than I'd felt in ages, then I settled down to see what was happening on Facebook. To my surprise I noticed a friend I hadn't heard from in ages had put up a post. She'd been distracted for months she explained as her father had had cancer, but now, thanks to a wonderful doctor, he was improving at last, so full of good news, she was back online.

I stared at the words in amazement. This was surely not a coincidence. It must be what we call pure synchronicity – meaningful events sent to us out of the blue that we should take notice of. Instantly I knew what I had to do. I grabbed my phone and quickly punched in my friend's number. After a quick greeting and saying how pleased I was to hear her father was doing so well, I asked if she could share the name of the doctor who'd worked such wonders for her dad. Of course, she was happy to pass it on. Turned out the man was a private consultant based in Harley Street. I phoned him immediately and to my surprise, he happened to be in the office at that very moment and agreed to speak to me.

'I can't promise anything,' he said finally, when I'd explained the situation – though I left out the bit about the spirit voice, 'But send me through your mother's clinical notes and I'll take a look at them. If I feel there's anything I can do, I'll let you know.'

Ecstatic, I arranged for Mum's notes to be forwarded to him. I was quite sure I'd found the answer. If it wasn't Mum's time to go, this must be the man who could help her stay with us.

Sure enough, a couple of days later he called me back to say he thought he could treat her. 'I can't cure her,' he said, 'but if she is willing to try chemotherapy there's a good chance we can extend her life. It has to be her decision though.'

'Of course,' I said and arranged a date to take Mum to see him.

Lorraine was concerned at the idea of chemotherapy – often a gruelling treatment – was it right to put a lady in her eighties through it she wondered? But Mum shrugged off all worries. It was her body and if there was a chance of keeping it going for a few more years, she was up for it.

She was happy to meet the new consultant and assured him she was prepared to try the fortnightly treatment he proposed, even if it did prove demanding. But at least there was some reassuring news. The consultant said it was very unlikely the medication he would be recommending would cause her to lose her hair – which had been one of Mum's main concerns about the treatment. Her lovely hair had been

Mum's pride and joy.

'Ok then,' said Mum, 'I'd like to give it a try.'

He smiled. 'Fine my dear. I'll make the arrangements. And I have to say, with that positive attitude, I expect to be dancing with you at your 90th birthday party!'

Mum of course thought he was charming. And it was true, he was a charming man, but best of all he gave her the gift of hope – unlike the other doctors who could only offer her gloom and their condolences.

So back into hospital she went. The treatment was long and gruelling as we'd been warned, but the consultant was as good as his word. Mum kept her hair, though it did thin a bit - but best of all, she did live to enjoy her 90th birthday party. In fact, she enjoyed several more bonus years on top, confounding the original doctors who'd been so pessimistic. What's more, one of the three best friends who'd been at tea that day did sadly pass away before her – just as the spirit voice had predicted.

As Mum grew stronger, my mind calmed and I decided to treat myself to a little break after all the stress. I booked myself on a three-day mini-cruise to Belgium – the exciting part for me being not so much the trip to Belgium but the fact it was a psychic development cruise, led by the famous medium Gordon Smith.

I had a great time. Gordon is an inspiring man, I made lots of new friends and as usual I ended up doing readings for some of my fellow passengers. One of them was particularly fascinating.

The lady in front of me came from a family that originated in London's East End – rather as mine had done, at one point. But what took my breath away was when the relative in spirit who stepped forward to communicate, showed me a wonderfully vivid scene. Suddenly I was staring at four magnificent black horses with great, black feather plumes on their heads, prancing in front of a gleaming black carriage that carried the coffin through the city streets.

'She's telling me she had the most splendid, traditional funeral,' I told my sitter, 'with horses, a carriage, the lot. A real show stopper!'

And as I stared at the scene, I got a close up of the words 'Mum', each letter spelled out individually in perfect white roses.

'Oh - it's your Mum!' I added.

'Yes that's right,' agreed the woman, 'She had a wonderful send off. And you should have seen the flowers!'

At which the Mum instantly switched the scene in my mind and showed me a heap of wreaths and banks of blooms piled up in the cemetery – enough to keep ten flower shops going for weeks. She was obviously a very popular lady.

She wanted her daughter to know there was no need to be sad she'd missed her granddaughter's wedding because she'd been there, and she particularly admired the beautiful roses in the bridal bouquet and the men's buttonholes. She'd also had a good laugh at the funny moment where the best man tripped over the bride's train in the church.

My fellow passenger was in tears and then in tears of laughter. The episode was so striking it stayed with me long after the cruise ended.

After that I think word of my shipboard readings must have got round because a little later I was invited on another cruise – to the Caribbean. This time not as a passenger but as a medium. It was another psychic cruise with various mediums including the Psychic Sisters from the London store Selfridges doing their thing, and I was tasked with running mediumship development workshops for the passengers who wanted to take part.

This is the life! I couldn't help thinking as we cruised by Key West in Florida and on to the Cayman-Islands over the impossibly blue Caribbean. Of course I was working, as well as having fun. So one afternoon midway through the cruise, I took advantage of a break in my time-table to slip away to the spa for a massage.

I love a massage. So relaxing. And this time was no different. As the young woman worked out the knots in my shoulders, and the sweet scent of the massage oil filled the air, I drifted blissfully away.

Then all at once I realised that me and the masseuse were no longer alone. I was looking at an elderly woman with a pink cardigan hugged round her shoulders.

'I'm her gran,' said the elderly woman – obviously a spirit woman, 'Tell her about the pink blanket. Pink's my favourite colour. They put my pink blanket in with me when I was buried, and I was wearing this cardigan. That's my granddaughter with you. She's got my gold wedding ring you know.'

For a few minutes I didn't move. This was awkward. I always tell my students that it's important to be disciplined. You mustn't stay open all the time to messages for everyone you meet. For a start it might be upsetting to spring such things on unsuspecting strangers who've not asked for a reading and secondly, it's not good for the medium to be working continuously.

Yet somehow during the massage I'd become so chilled, my inner message filter must have slipped. 'Tell her, tell her!' prompted the old lady when she realised I'd made no move to mention her to the masseuse.

'I can't just blurt it out,' I protested silently, 'She doesn't even know I do this sort of thing.'

'I only want her to know she's on the right path and I'm proud of her,' the old lady insisted.

So in the end I explained the situation to the young woman and passed on her grandmother's message. She was stunned, but fortunately, she took the surprising news very well. And yes, she confirmed, pink had been her grandmother's favourite colour and she was indeed buried wearing the cardigan I mentioned. And yes they'd even put Gran's favourite blanket in the coffin with her.

Then, tears in her eyes, the masseuse pulled down the neck of her tunic and pulled out the chain that was hanging round her neck. There swinging on the end was her grandma's golden wedding-ring.

'I never take it off,' she said.

Afterwards, on the way back to my cabin I realised I should have been prepared for a spirit approach during a massage. I'd almost forgotten but it had happened before, during a massage on a holiday in Cape Verde.

On that occasion, while I was floating away, almost asleep as the woman worked, a young man glided into my mind. He had drowned at sea, he told me. His boat had capsized and he was trapped under the water.

The masseuse was his sister he explained and he wanted her to know he was ok.

'I'm still around her,' he said, 'I know about her little boy. I've been watching him grow up. I know how she struggles to make ends meet.' And he showed me how hard she had to work to feed the child. 'Tell her things will get easier,' he said.

He was so insistent I pass the message on, I couldn't relax. He nagged and nagged at me. Yet I had to wait till the masseuse finished before I could try to explain. She didn't speak a lot of English and I don't think she quite understood what a medium did. But eventually it dawned on her that I was trying to tell her her brother was still close – lived on in spirit in fact and was sending his love. She was quite overcome and ended up smothering me with grateful hugs. So on this occasion it was a good thing I'd let my filter slip.

Back home from my travels, Mum continued to stay well – albeit with fortnightly chemo sessions - and I threw myself into my teaching and private readings. Usually I see a wide variety of people with a wide variety of issues but around this time I began to notice something slightly odd was happening. Over and over again the same problem seemed to present itself. Woman after woman stuck in an unsatisfactory relationship seemed to find their way to my door.

It was only when Suzanne – the latest in a long line – sat down at my little basement table, I began to realise what spirit was trying to tell me.

Suzanne was hoping to contact her mother. And luckily her mother came straight through. And it soon became clear that Suzanne's marriage was not very happy.

'It's not been right for years,' she explained, 'We stayed together for the sake of the children, but the children have left home now. I'm comfortable enough and my husband's not a bad man – but we're living a lie. I feel I should move out to be true to myself... but I'm scared... What does my mum think I should do?'

As I recall, her mum advised her not be scared and if she was that unhappy, to make a new life for herself. But after Suzanne had gone I realised her mum's message was also a message for me. I knew in theory that when the spirit world wants to teach you a lesson, if you ignore it, they keep representing the lesson, over and over until you get it. Could it be this was happening to me?

I thought back to that woman long ago who shocked me by saying she so loathed her husband she wanted to stick pins in his eyes – yet she stayed with him. And all the similar women who'd come through my door since. Now their numbers were increasing.

Was this a lesson for me? I thought of Simon and the way our interests had diverged. I realised that for years I'd been trying to ignore the fact that increasingly, we were living in different worlds. I couldn't close my eyes to it any longer. And while we weren't at each other's throats, we weren't on the same wavelength either. The children had gone, the connection between us had gone; really, we had very little left in common.

When we got married all those years before, in my young, idealistic way I thought it would be forever. Yet now I knew that sometimes, there are people who come into your life for a reason and walk alongside you for a time, a very important time, but then your paths take you in different directions and you both move on.

Looking at my marriage realistically, I had to admit that that's what had happened to Simon and me. To pretend to myself otherwise was a lie. Like Suzanne, it was time to be true to myself and start a whole new chapter – as an independent woman. I will always love Simon and value the years we had together, but it was time for us to go our separate ways.

My first visit to the Arthur Findlay College and the giant orb (top left) which joined me in the garden!

Me and David - reconnecting 'Andy Cap' at the Arthur Findlay College

Meeting Simon Cowell at a Charity fundraiser

My 50th birthday - Burlesque style!

Visiting Salem, USA and the Witch Museum!

*Another course - I can't get enough!
Outside the wonderful Arthur Findlay College*

Proud to be part of a Psychic Caribbean Cruise

As spiritual as a girl can be - I still love those sparkly shoes!

Teaching a workshop my own style!

Mum feeling 'at home' on a balcony on holiday in Spain

THIRTEEN:
How lovely to live in a house touched by angels...

I stared at the estate agent's details in my hand. 'Angel Cottages' read the title above a photograph of a town house at the end of a row.

It wasn't at all what I was looking for. I'd asked the agents to let me know about any older, character properties that came on their books. I was thinking converted barns, oak beams, log-burners – that sort of thing. I didn't even mind about location.

Since Simon and I had split, we finally sold our lovely home in Hertfordshire. It was a massive wrench and I was sad to leave but it had to be done. I'd moved into a rented house with my two dogs and began to search far and wide for my perfect new pad as an independent woman.

I'd put my name down at estate agents in several counties and travelled far and wide, exploring remote villages and visiting all manner of pretty homes. I'd actually even made up my mind to buy one lovely barn conversion on the edge of a hamlet in north Bedfordshire, but then I'd taken Mum to see it and she burst into tears. There was nothing wrong with the property, it was just she couldn't bear to think of me being so far away. Admittedly it was over an hour's drive from her retirement flat but I like driving and I felt the journey was quite manageable.

Mum didn't see it the same way of course. It seemed like the ends of the earth to her. Plus: 'There's no Jewish shops,' she said,' And where's the deli to get your cholla?' She was talking about the special bread that Jews eat on the Sabbath and special holidays.

There wasn't a week went by when I didn't buy one for her. She was wonderfully set in her traditional ways.

She assured me bravely that she wouldn't want to stop me buying the house I wanted and of course she agreed the barn I'd chosen was very nice. Yet it was quite clear she was unhappy and if Mum was unhappy, how could I be happy? So I dithered and procrastinated – and then along came the latest suggestion from the estate agent.

I stared again at the photograph of the Angel Cottages house. It was nothing like the sort of place I'd requested. It wasn't old, it didn't have oak beams and there wasn't a log-burner in sight. And yet! There was something about it that drew me in. Even the name seemed like a sign. Happy clients often called me an angel – which always made me smile because I didn't feel the least angelic. But how lovely to live in a house touched by angels! I looked at the rest of the address. It was also a much easier drive to Mum's – so she'd be pleased… The only problem was it was out of my price range.

Nevertheless, it couldn't hurt to go and have a look, could it? And as soon as I pulled up outside, I knew. Set in a quiet lane overlooking a little green complete with duck pond, the house was modern, yet quirky. Spread over four floors it had a compact, courtyard style garden at the back and on the middle floor a spacious balcony seemingly right in the treetops of the big wooded garden that curled around behind the cottages. Sitting on that balcony watching the birds come and go must be like living in a tree-house I thought. Above all, the place felt warm and welcoming. The atmosphere had wrapped around me, comfortable and safe, as soon as I walked in the door. I could be at home here I thought.

Apparently the modern cottages were named for the pub that once stood on the site – the Angel Inn I believe. Even the pond was called Angel Pond. Call me fanciful but it seemed like a sign to me.

There was the tricky problem of the price of course, but the spirit world had that covered too. It turned out that asbestos was found in the building as well as other problems, so the owners agreed to reduce the price to allow for essential building work to make the place safe.

It took over six months to get everything done and during that time my sister was kind enough to let me and the dogs stay with her. But at last, just around Christmas I was able to move in. I had everything I needed, right down to a spiritual-room where I could do my readings, cleverly created from the integral garage.

Nice as it would have been to have a garage, there was space to park my car outside the house, so converting the garage to a dedicated room for my readings was much more useful. And what a good job the builder did. I told him about the time, years before when I'd attended a séance at the Arthur Findlay College and clairvoyantly saw little lights twinkling all over the ceiling just like the night sky, as the medium worked – and the description seemed to inspire him.

'Leave it to me!' said the builder. 'I know just what to do.'

He painted the ceiling midnight-sky black and covered it with tiny little pinhole lights to represent stars. Then he coloured the walls purple, overlaid with a shimmering, semi-transparent wash. The effect was calming, yet other-worldly. I loved it.

I loved working there, but sadly not long afterwards I had to abandon my dreams of becoming a tutor at the Arthur Findlay College once and for all.

The decision came about quite unexpectedly. By this time. I'd taken the plunge and started attending college courses again. Upsetting though the misunderstanding and threat of appearing before the tribunal had been, I still loved the place and as the years went by and the memories of that episode became less raw, I calmed down enough to consider going back.

Admittedly I was nervous as I walked back through Stansted Hall's big oak door, unsure of the reception I'd receive but fortunately everyone was as welcoming as ever and the incident seemed to have been forgotten.

In fact, it was all going so well, I decided to resume studying for the qualification that would enable me to become an Arthur Findlay tutor. I re-joined the SNU and began to look forward to the day when I too might be welcoming my own students to the college.

So far so good I thought. But then several visits later, a group of us were chatting over drinks in the bar after the Sunday service one day when somehow it came up that I was Jewish. This seemed to puzzle one of the new tutors particularly as I had been saying excitedly that I was training to be a college tutor too.

'Surely you can't be a tutor or member of the SNU if you're Jewish,' they said, 'You have to be a Spiritualist.'

'Well I am,' I said, 'but I'm Jewish too and I've already paid my deposit for the course.'

'You can't be,' they persisted, 'Spiritualism's a religion and you can't have two religions.'

'Well I believe in all the teachings of Spiritualism,' I said.

'So you can't be Jewish then,' they insisted.

'But I am,' I said. 'I was born Jewish.'

There was no answer to that. We were going round in circles and the subject was dropped. Yet afterwards the conversation troubled me so much I went off to find one of the course organisers to check.

'Bev,' he said, when I explained what had been said. 'They're right. You can't have two religions. If you want to be a member of the SNU you have to be a Spiritualist, so you'll need to give up being Jewish.'

'But surely, Maurice Barbanell was Jewish,' I said.

We heard a lot about the late Maurice Barbanell at the college. He was revered as one of the great pioneers of

Spiritualism. He was a gifted medium who'd also helped found the magazine Psychic News and became its first editor in 1932. He'd even met the legendary Arthur Findlay back then and persuaded him to invest in the publication.

In later years he was invited to give a talk to the college at Stansted Hall, I believe and ever since, we students have been told of his valuable contribution to the movement.

Yet Maurice was Jewish.

Not that I was comparing myself to the great Mr Barbanell of course, but even so. If one of our heroes was Jewish, surely it wouldn't hurt if I kept the religion of my birth? The tutor shook his head, clearly unimpressed with my line of reasoning. 'Doesn't matter Bev,' he insisted, 'that's the rule.'

I was horrified. It would break my mother's heart if I renounced my Jewish faith. The Jewish festivals and traditions were an integral part of our family and extended family life. They were especially important to mum and my two children. There was no way I could turn my back on them.

I agonised over the dilemma for weeks. I was still able to study at the college whatever my religion of course, but I so wanted to teach there. Yet in order to teach, I had to be a member of the SNU and to be a member of the SNU, I had to give up my Jewish faith. It was Catch 22.

Eventually I realised I had no choice. I couldn't be a hypocrite. It would have been so easy to pretend I was now exclusively a Spiritualist, but that wouldn't be true and it wouldn't be right to lie. I am Jewish in my heart and a

Spiritualist in my head. So when membership renewal time came round again I made one last check about the rules, just in case anything had changed. But it was confirmed. I would need to give up my Jewish faith and become exclusively a Spiritualist in order to be a member. So with a heavy heart, I had to decline. I said a sad goodbye to the SNU and all hopes of teaching at the college.

Now I was on my own, with a future to rethink.

FOURTEEN:

Sparkly boots featured in every window… it was destiny!

I looked at my watch. Oops… how had it got so late so soon? My client would be here any minute. In fact, was that a car drawing up outside right now?

Fortunately, my workroom was all prepared. Candles lit, atmosphere calm.

I tidied my hair with a last quick brush, pulled on my sparkly boots and hurried down to open the door.

It might sound odd but those sparkly boots – or sometimes glittery shoes – had become an integral part of my preparations. Despite the fact that once, a tutor at the college had told us students we must dress quietly and avoid all flamboyance in our clothing, hair and make-up as the spirits disapproved of such trappings as distracting and unappealing, I found that my own delight in a touch of glitz didn't seem to bother them at all. In fact, in honour of my new, sparkly surroundings I'd got into the habit of putting on my sparkly boots before starting work, just to set the mood.

I've always liked a bit of sparkle of course but my current phase of eye-catching footwear came about after a trip to Dublin. A friend had kindly bought me tickets for my birthday to see the famous American medium John Edward who was appearing in the city. It was a wonderful treat and John Edward was fascinating, but oddly enough, my lasting reminder of the trip was a wonderful pair of sparkly boots.

The unintended purchase was a complete accident. My friend and I were whiling away the time before John's show, wandering up and down Dublin's shopping streets and I couldn't help noticing that sparkly boots seemed to feature in every other window. I'm not sure why there were so many. Perhaps it was the latest Irish fashion craze. But whatever the reason, I heartily approved. Anything that glitters always catches my eye and I was entranced. I immediately wanted a pair to take home.

Trouble was they were incredibly expensive and I didn't know whether I could justify the extravagance.

Then, turning a corner, we suddenly found ourselves in a smaller, quieter street and there, right at the front of the window of a modest shop was an even more gorgeous pair of boots; shimmering in pinks, silvers and blues. What's more they were half the price of their flashy sisters round the corner.

What could I do? It was destiny! In I went to try them on and they were so comfortable, there was no turning back. That evening as I watched John Edward weaving his magic on the stage, I was also sneaking admiring peeps at my glamorous feet, sparkling quietly in their new wonder-boots under the seat.

Perhaps it was because I associated the boots with a splendid psychic evening, who knows? - but somehow, after that, I got into the habit of putting them on every time I did a reading. Since then, numerous similar pairs have joined my collection, along with various sets of glittering shoes. I'm not sure if my spirit visitors actually appreciate them, just tolerate them or don't even notice, but they certainly help get me in the right frame of mind!

Gradually, as well as readings, I set up my own workshops and mentoring sessions from my new home and it soon became clear my spiritual work in Angel Cottages was developing and expanding. The strange thing was my readings had a knack of providing me with valuable lessons to pass on to my students – so one side of my work, complemented the other perfectly. Well, I say strange, but it's not really odd. As I've learned by now, that's the way the spirit world organises things. If you're meant to do something, everything falls easily into place.

I began to get used to the different ways my spirit communicators would present themselves. On one occasion I was reading for a woman and her father came through. Yet oddly I picked up a mental picture of my own Uncle Paul. I was puzzled but thought I'd go along with it.

'I have a man here whose name is Paul,' I said.

'Yes that's right,' she said.

'And he had a problem with his mind towards the end?' I asked because that's what happened to my Uncle Paul.

'Yes he did,' she confirmed. 'He had dementia.'

Then I saw Uncle Paul in his taxi because before he got sick, he was a taxi driver.

'He's in a taxi - would you understand he's a taxi driver?'

'Yes he was!' she assured me, amazed.

Now I understood. They'd shown me my own Uncle Paul as a form of spiritual shorthand, because of the striking similarities between the two men. It was the quickest way of putting me on the right track. I've noticed they often use personal images and memories from your own mind to help you make sense of what they're trying to tell you.

Yet despite this, there's sometimes a temptation for the medium to try too hard which invariably ends up with the reading taking a wrong turn. It happens because it's such a good feeling to get detail after detail of evidence correct, that you want to go on pleasing the client by giving them all the info they would like. Yet you can't make demands on the spirit world.

Some clients arrive with a list of specific people they want to speak to and no one else will do. Others think we can summon up the departed celebrity of their choice, a person they never knew in life, because they'd always fancied a chat with them.

John Lennon anyone? Princess Diana? I have to explain it can't be done. The spirit has to want to come forward to speak to them, not the other way round and why would John Lennon or the Princess want to drop in to say hello to someone they'd never met?

Other clients hope for specific information that the spirit world is reluctant to provide. And who knows, there may be very good reasons why it's not in the best interests of the client to find out certain details at that particular moment, much as they think they want to know. Then again, clients sometimes want to find out about matters that are none of their business.

Once I was giving a reading to a middle aged lady and it was going tremendously. Five of her loved ones were eager to talk to her and she was blown away by the communications. We had her mother, father, grandmother, brother and even a friend – all dropping in during the session. With each positive piece of evidence, the energy was getting stronger and stronger and the lady was delighted.

But then she said, 'Can you tell me about my son? Can you get anything for him?'

I faltered. 'How old is your son?' I asked.

'Thirty-two,' she said.

This threw me. I wanted to do as she asked but I knew it wasn't a good idea. 'As he's an adult,' I explained, 'he really needs his own reading. It's not right to delve into another adult's private life.'

But she was disappointed and I hated to disappoint her, so I tried.

Well it all went wrong. The more I strained and struggled to force some info out, the more incorrect my comments became. I could feel the vibrant energy we'd generated earlier draining away, and I realised it was my own mind supplying the pitiful scraps I came out with, not the spirit world. If I was not careful, I'd undo all the good work achieved at the beginning of the reading and she'd go away remembering only the unsuccessful attempts.

In my mind's eye I could see the woman's mother still hovering close. 'Listen you've got to help me out here.' I implored her silently, 'Your daughter's desperate for something about her son. She was so pleased before, and now she's likely to go away with doubts, because I can't tell her anything about him.'

To my relief the mum came to the rescue.

'She's worried about the boy because he's spending beyond his means,' she said, 'He's just gone out and bought a new BMW. Silver it is. And the registration number is…' and she spelled it out. 'He can't afford it. He's always doing things like that. He'll get in trouble if he's not careful.'

'Thank you!' I said, then I turned to my client. 'Your mother's telling me your son badly needs to reign in his spending,' I said. 'He's bought a car he can't afford – a silver BMW and the number plate is: …' and I repeated the registration numbers and letters I'd been given.

The woman's mouth fell open. 'How in the world…did you get that?' she gasped. 'That's exactly right!'

'Well his grandmother's concerned about him. She knows what's going on,' I said. 'So do tell him what she said.'

And with that I quickly brought the reading to a close. I'd

learned a valuable lesson that day, a lesson I passed onto my students. Stick to what the spirit communicators want to tell you – don't be tempted to stray into other areas – no matter how much your client tries to persuade you to do otherwise.

Sometimes of course, it's the other way round. Sometimes a spirit wishes to communicate with a person who has no desire to talk to them.

I remember one young woman who sat herself down a shade nervously at my little table, clearly unsure what to expect. Almost immediately I sensed a male presence coming forward. I was just opening my mouth to tell her about him when I was stopped short by the image that suddenly appeared in my mind. The man was showing me a big, brown leather belt.

It could have been his favourite item of clothing, or perhaps a gift she'd given him but there was something about it that chilled me to the bone. I just knew before he admitted it, he'd used that belt to beat her with. He was the young woman's father and he'd come back to say how sorry he was for abusing his only daughter when she was a child.

This was a very delicate situation. I could tell the young woman had no wish to be reunited with her father. She was probably relieved when he did the family a favour and passed away. She certainly didn't want to think of him hanging around now he was supposed to be gone.

Yet confronted on arriving in the spirit world with a true understanding of the effect of his violence, the father was now desperate to be forgiven by his daughter.

I had to tell him this may not be possible. Quite a few people are not ready to forgive, just because their departed relative wants them to, and it's not fair to try to persuade them.

In the end we compromised. I agreed to explain to the daughter that her dad was truly sorry so that however she felt about him, at least she would know now and would always know, he was contrite. This satisfied the father.

Then afterwards I helped the daughter with a guided meditation to cut the ties that still bound her to the hurt and trauma of the past.

When she finally left, it was like a weight she didn't even know she was carrying, had been lifted from her shoulders. The reading wasn't what she'd expected but as it turned out, it was what she needed.

It's surprising how often spirits who've passed over do want to speak to those they've hurt but it's not always appropriate.

Once, I'd popped into a nail-bar to get my nails smartened up. There I was, happily watching the glorious splash of colour sliding over my nails when a young man started tugging at my mind. He tried to insist I told the technician working at the next table that George was here. 'Go on, go on, tell her it's George,' he pestered. He even wanted me to nudge her to attract her attention.

But I wouldn't. I had a feeling the technician wouldn't welcome this news. She hadn't sought out a medium as far as I knew and she no doubt thought she'd heard the last from George long ago. As far as she was concerned George was dead and buried. Seemed to me, for her sake, it was best to keep it that way.

And you always have to remember that whatever you tell someone could stay with them for the rest of their life. So you have to take personal responsibility for what you say.

I'll never forget the time while Simon and I were still together when we decided to take a last minute break at a health spa. We wanted to forget about work and unwind for a couple of days but wouldn't you know it? As soon as we checked in we noticed a poster on the wall advertising that evening's entertainment – a talk about the psychic world!

'Talk about a busman's holiday,' said Simon ruefully.

He wasn't madly keen but I felt it would be rude not to go – the least I could do was show a fellow medium a bit of support.

The evening went well enough but what really got my attention was the question and answer session at the end. Or at least, one question in particular.

'Can you tell me if there's anything I can do to speed things up?' this lady in the centre of the room asked. 'I was told by a psychic 33 years ago that I had 36 years of bad luck in front of me. Well I've had 33 years so far and there's three years left to go. Is there anything I can do to get rid of the bad luck right now?'

I can't recall now exactly how the medium answered but I was absolutely horrified. For a start I don't believe in such things. I believe our thoughts create our reality so fearing negative events and sending out negative thoughts all the time will draw towards you exactly the kind of negative luck you're hoping to avoid. It then becomes a self-fulfilling prophecy.

I was outraged that more than three decades ago some irresponsible, so-called psychic could have taken it upon herself to give this woman such a devastating prediction. That poor client had carried those words around with her for thirty-three years. They were still as fresh in her mind as the day they were uttered and no doubt had blighted her life ever since. Yet it was complete rubbish.

I couldn't help myself. I stood up and added my two penn'orth.

'You need to think positive,' I assured the lady, 'Let go of that 36 year prediction. Send it away with love and from now on think positive thoughts.'

All she had to do was keep focusing on the good things in her world and gradually she would draw happy things towards her.

I came away from our weekend break more convinced than ever that I must weigh up every word before I opened my mouth when giving a reading to clients.

You also have to be especially tactful when you're demonstrating in public to an audience. It would be so easy to blurt out everything you see and hear but you have to bear in mind that the recipient might be embarrassed in front of a crowd of strangers. So sometimes you have to choose your words with great care.

I remember once being confronted by a spirit lady who was without doubt one of the ugliest women I'd ever seen. She was a delightful soul but sadly in life had clearly not been blessed in the looks department. She had a huge hook nose, with a pimple on the end, a bent back and for some reason, she was holding an apple. She looked exactly like the wicked witch in the Disney movie, Snow White.

I stared down at her grand-daughter, waiting eagerly in the audience for whatever I might be about to tell her. How was I going to describe her loved one in a way that wouldn't upset her?

'Ummm I've got a lady here,' I began uneasily, 'with a very… distinguished… nose. In fact, it's one of her most… striking… features. And for some reason, she's showing me an apple.'

At this the grand-daughter hooted with laughter. Fortunately, she wasn't at all embarrassed.

'Don't worry. I know what you mean,' she said, 'My gran looked like a witch! She was really ugly. She had this big, hooked nose with a spot on the end! But she did. She looked like a witch!'

'She is showing me an apple,' I continued, very relieved she was taking it so well.

'She worked in a greengrocer's,' said the grand-daughter, 'she used to polish up the apples till they shone, to make them look more appealing.'

Once again I marvelled at the cleverness of the spirit people.

Though she was now a beautiful soul, the grandmother had rapidly established her identity for her grand-daughter simply by giving me a quick view of her extraordinary nose – her most distinguishing feature in life - along with a symbol of her old job.

And of course spirit people don't suddenly become all pious and prudish when they move on. They retain the personalities we knew and loved when they were on the earth plane, so you have to be prepared to be told absolutely anything!

During one demonstration another feisty mum stepped forward. Most spirits like to explain how they came to pass over, as this helps identify them. This lady was no exception but I couldn't quite understand what she was trying to tell me.

She kept indicating her thighs, around her stocking-tops and was making an odd jiggling movement.

After a while I had an idea of what she was trying to communicate, but: 'I can't say that!' I told her out loud.

She laughed and carried on, jiggling more vigorously, 'No I'm not saying that!' I insisted.

By now the audience was calling out, demanding to know what I was hearing.

'No, no I really can't,' I said. 'I'll tell you later,' I added to her daughter and grand-daughter who were right in front of me.

After the demonstration the two women came round to say hello.

'I know what you were trying to say!' the mum said, not at all upset. 'My mother died while making love.'

Her own daughter gasped in surprise. 'I never knew grandma died like that!' she said, rather shocked.

Exactly. This is why you can't just come out with very personal details in front of an audience.

Still, it's good to know the old lady went out on a high!

FIFTEEN:

Right by my foot was the little golden heart...

I stared at my classmate. We were at the college and once again we'd been asked to work in pairs. So Carol was sitting there in front of me, relaxed and oblivious, but behind her, quite clearly I could see the tall, imposing figure of a woman in a nurse's uniform of the first World War. She was dressed in a long skirt, there was a starched white cap on her head and she wore a full length apron with a red cross on the bib.

She smiled a kindly smile in Carol's direction and nodded encouragingly to me. In her face I could see enormous patience and great wisdom. I knew instantly that she was my friend's spirit guide.

'Carol,' I began, 'I've got your guide here. She's a nurse. A nurse from long ago. She's standing right behind you.'

To my surprise, Carol began to cry.

'You don't know how much that means to me,' she sniffed, searching in her pockets for a tissue. 'I know my guide's a nurse, I've seen her many times. It's so good to have it verified by someone else – and to know she's close by.'

I was only too pleased to have been able to help. I remember how thrilled I was when I first saw my own guide – the Knight on horseback – that day at my development circle.

Since then I've learned a lot more about guides of course. They are highly evolved spirits who help us on our journey and they are with us before we're born, to plan what we need to learn in this current lifetime. Once we've arrived on earth as a tiny baby we tend to forget everything that has gone before, so our guides stay close to us throughout our human experience to help us stay on our chosen path and give us a little nudge now and then. They also assist in taking you back to spirit when you die.

Actually I've been told we're likely to have quite a variety of guides popping in along the way, at different stages of our journey. They come to assist with various aspects of your life in order that you learn and grow.

Since I met my Knight who's my main guide, Arthur, I've also met a native American Indian, a Tibetan monk and a Roman Gladiator who all turn up to aid me now and then when I need different types of help. I see them in mind's eye and I can feel their presence. Each has a different role to play.

And in recent years I've even solved the mystery of those strange, transparent globes that used to float around my childhood bedroom. At development circle I learned they're referred to as 'orbs' – little bubbles of spirit energy that come close, to let you know they're there. You can sometimes see them in broad daylight as well as at night and they often show up unexpectedly in photographs. When they appear this way they can cause quite a bit of consternation to the unsuspecting photographer who thinks the camera must be faulty, as no orbs were visible when they took the picture.

But amazingly, the orbs *were* there when the picture was taken – it was just that the photographer couldn't see them! For some strange reason the camera frequently captures these different wavelengths that most of us are unable to see with the naked eye.

These days, now I'm no longer nervous of orbs, I've become so fascinated by them I often grab my phone and photograph them and video them when they appear to me. They come in all shapes and sizes and colours. Some even have faces in them which have been captured on a screenshot. Incredible.

The other amazing thing about energy is that it's around us all the time. You know when you walk into a room or a building and sense an atmosphere? And not always a nice atmosphere at that? It's simply left-behind energy from other people's emotions that at some point, they've unknowingly let loose in the room. The stronger the emotion released, the longer it may last. Which is why particularly sensitive people may feel uncomfortable or scared in places where tragic or violent events have occurred, sometimes centuries ago. Yet there's no need to be frightened. However spooked you may feel, the energy can't harm you. The most damaging effect is more likely to be the stress caused by your own fears.

On the other hand, the opposite sometimes occurs. Certain places exude a wonderfully calm, peaceful energy. They draw people to them to soak up the tranquillity. Perhaps highly spiritual personalities lived or worked in these settings over the years and they too have left behind the atmosphere they created. These special buildings or landscapes often become places of pilgrimage. Visitors go away refreshed and recharged just by spending a little time absorbing all those positive vibes.

I've learned so much over the years. I know now that no one comes into your life by accident. Everyone you meet or spend time with is there for a reason. Some stay for years, others for a few months or even the briefest encounter. You each learn what you need to learn from the other and then move on when you've fulfilled your task.

I found this idea immensely comforting whenever I thought about the breakdown of my marriage to Simon because I'd cried so many tears for years afterwards. Simon was my best friend and partner for 33 years since we'd first met. Every time our anniversary comes round in September I can't help remembering the many happy years we spent together and our two wonderful children. I'm sad it's over but clearly, we'd achieved what we set out to achieve when we planned it all before we were born. Naturally we had no idea of this when we first fell in love, but somehow we must have been destined to part.

For some couples of course, it's just the opposite. These are souls who have opted to remain working together for almost an entire lifetime. That's why they're often known as soulmates. Although they are unaware of it when they meet, they have joint tasks to perform and lessons to learn in this lifetime that will take them many years in each other's company to accomplish.

I met one of these special couples not long ago when Derek Robertson, a retired engineer from Devon contacted me for a reading. Derek was inconsolable after losing his beloved wife Anne, who'd been by his side for over half a century. In fact, they'd been together since falling in love at the age of just 15. Teenage sweethearts, they'd gone through life hand in hand until the dreadful time a couple of years ago when Anne sadly passed away with cancer.

Anne, who was a retired nurse, turned out to be a lively lady and a brilliant communicator. Theirs is such a wonderful love story I'll let Derek tell you what happened himself.

'When the doctors told Anne they couldn't do any more for her, we cried all the way home,' recalled Derek, 'She so wanted to be here to celebrate our 60th wedding anniversary, but it wasn't to be. After she died I read all the Doris Stokes books and found them so comforting I decided I must try to get a reading to see if I could contact Anne. Doris was no longer here of course but I found Bev and I went on to have several readings with her – the first, in November, the anniversary of Anne's death.

'Strangely enough when Bev got started she didn't get Anne immediately, she said she had a man there. He was showing her a tunnel, she said, he gave her the name Bob and he spoke with a Geordie accent.

'Well that amazed me because Anne's father was a Geordie named Bob and he was a coal miner. The tunnel made complete sense.

'Then Bev got Anne and even got her name. 'She's saying to me: 'We were like Tweedle Dum and Tweedle Dee – always together,' said Bev. 'You fitted together like a hand in a glove.' Which was true.

'Bev asked her how long we'd been married. I jumped in and said 58 years but Bev shook her head. 'I'm getting 57 years from Anne,' she said. And of course she was right. We'd been married 57 years when Anne died, but another year had gone by since then so I considered our marriage to be 58 years.'

'There were so many little details that were right. She mentioned my favourite meal was sausage and mash, she mentioned the Lake District, where we used to visit often. She also said that Anne had suffered a miscarriage early in our marriage – which was true – but that she'd met our son, now grown up in the spirit world. The baby had been a boy and he was called Philip she said.

'She also knew what I was doing. She said my sock drawer needed tidying – true, Anne used to do that for me. 'And why is she showing me your hair?' said Bev. 'She's behind you doing something with your hair.' I knew what she meant. She was brushing my hair. She did that every day.

'She also says she's been watching you writing letters and sticking down envelopes,' said Bev.

'Which was amazing because just the day before the reading I'd sat down with a stack of correspondence I'd been putting off for weeks because Anne used to deal with all that, and spent a lot of time sorting it out and getting it ready to post.

'She also scolded me because I'd stopped taking my pills – which was true – and made me promise to start again because she wanted me to look after myself.

'What about the dog?' I asked, 'Has she found our dog over there?'

'Yes,' said Bev, 'in fact I can see a golden retriever sitting with you, actually sitting on your feet!'

Right again. Our dog Kayla was a golden retriever and she always used to sit on my feet to keep them warm.

Then I asked Bev if she could get my special nickname for Anne. She looked a bit puzzled at first. 'It sounds like Big Fat Bon Bon…' said Bev. Very, very close. It was actually Big Fat Pud! Which might sound strange to others but it was affectionately meant and it always made Anne laugh.

'Over the next couple of readings more impressive details came out that there's no way Bev could have known. At one point she said: 'She's showing me her legs, keeps kicking her legs up and pushing a wheelchair away.' Well Anne was proud of her lovely legs and disappointed to have to use a wheelchair towards the end. She was trying to show me she was back on her feet again.

'She's telling me you were very patient with her when she was ill,' Bev went on, 'She says you helped her on with her shoes. Oh, and what's she showing me now? As you're putting on her shoes - are you tickling her toes and singing or something?'

'I knew exactly what she meant. When I helped Anne on with her socks and shoes I used to play with her toes, repeating the old rhyme to make her laugh: 'This little piggy went to market, this little piggy stayed at home…' Twiddling each toe as I got to a different piggy.

'Anne even seemed to know what was going on at home.

'She's telling me there are two red jumpers on the end of your bed,' Bev said. 'Two!' Which was quite right. I'd taken two out – one plain red, the other red with a pattern. I couldn't decide which one to wear and ended up leaving both on the bed and putting on something else! They were still there and Anne knew it.

'But perhaps the most amazing of all was when I asked Bev if Anne could give me a sign that she was close. Bev went quiet for a bit then: 'She says there will be a sign. But not yet. You'll get your sign on Christmas Day.'

'I couldn't think what it might be and Christmas Day began just like any other. I noticed nothing out of the ordinary. But then later, my son and daughter in law dropped in a Christmas present. When I opened it I couldn't believe my eyes. Before she became too ill, Anne had been working on a tapestry of a two elephants, a mum and baby, but she was unable to finish it.

'After she died, unbeknown to me, my daughter in law had taken the tapestry home and had been working on it ever since. She finished it, framed it and gave it to me for Christmas. When I opened the parcel and saw what it was, I cried. I knew immediately it was my sign.'

It's interesting to hear how important the sign was to Derek because the great thing about signs is that we can all receive them. You don't have to be a medium or a psychic to get a sign from the spirit world. All you have to do is ask – and be patient. You might not get a sign in the next few hours but eventually you'll see something meaningful or out of the ordinary and you'll just know.

Signs come in many forms. We've all heard about little white angel feathers that can appear, seemingly out of nowhere to reassure us our loved ones are close. Some people associate robins with departed loved ones, others, coins.

Once, I was doing a reading for a woman and her mother came through. The mother wanted her daughter to know she was sending a sign. She told her she would find a coin in her bedroom when she got home. Well the daughter searched high and low when she got back but there was no coin anywhere. Disappointed she finally went to bed. The next morning when she woke up something made her lift her pillow. There underneath, was a shiny new penny.

Talk about pennies from Heaven!

Other signs take a more literal form. Driving home on the motorway one night from another residential course at the college I was deliberating over whether it was too extravagant for me to book up for a return course in a few weeks' time. It was a bit close to the course I'd just done, but the tutor was my favourite, Glyn Edwards. I was very tempted. So should I or shouldn't I, I wondered.

'If I should do the course,' I said aloud to the spirits, 'Show me a star!'

Since it was a filthy night with thick cloud, rain splashing down and my windscreen wipers going full tilt there wasn't much chance of the murk clearing and stars appearing, I thought.

But just then, a big tanker pulled out behind me and started to overtake. As it thundered alongside, I saw the words 'Texaco' written along the tanker's flank next to a big red star. I'd got my answer. The course it was!

Some-time later I was telling this story to my new students. 'I find that too hard to believe,' said one of the young men.

'Well just give it a try. Just ask.'

A few days later he phoned me. 'You'll never guess what happened,' he said.

Apparently his late father had been a fishmonger. 'I was driving along the motorway and said: 'If you're there Dad, give me a sign,' the young man said. 'A few minutes later a lorry went by and as it drew level I saw a logo design of a fish just above the wheel-arch. I couldn't believe it. That was a sign alright!'

Okay, you can dismiss these things as coincidences, but leaving aside the fact I don't believe in coincidences – they're synchronicities as I like to think of them - in the context in which these things happened, they felt exactly like signs, to the people who experienced them.

So why not give it a try? Ask any question you like. Which pathway shall I take? Should I accept the job I've been offered? Is this the partner for me? It's amazing how an answer can often appear in the most unexpected places. Often you'll switch on the radio and find the lyrics of a song that suddenly bursts out contain the answer to your question. Or you'll see a number plate that contains the letters of a relevant name. Sometimes a book will fall open on a page with something meaningful to your situation. It might even fall off the shelf at your feet.

The most incredible example that happened to me occurred when I was having coffee with a friend to discuss a series of workshops we were planning to do together. We happened to be sitting by the window of the coffee shop and as we talked, I glanced up and noticed a truck go by. On the side was written: 'Go for it!' Behind, followed another truck plastered with the words: 'The World is Your Oyster', then came another: 'Are you ready?' I started to laugh. This was crazy. Talk about a message! Finally, the last truck thundered by and on the side in huge letters was the name: 'Higginson'.

I was gobsmacked. There was no doubt in my mind that Gordon Higginson was letting us know he supported our venture. Me and my friend had a good laugh about it. And we went on to have a very successful series of workshops.

It's very strange, but signs are all around and you'll know one when you see it even though to anyone else, it will appear completely meaningless.

Some time after my father died, my sister phoned in quite a bit of distress. We both regularly visited his grave and for many months we'd had a little gold badge in the shape of a heart placed on his carved stone memorial prayer book. When the weather was windy we even taped it in place so it couldn't blow away. It had been there for ages but now, Lorraine said, when she'd gone along for her usual visit, the little heart had vanished. She'd searched all around the grave and surrounding area but it was nowhere to be seen.

We were both upset about it but fortunately I was going to the cemetery soon myself. 'I do hope someone hasn't taken it,' I said, 'I'll have a good look as well when I get there.'

So, the following week when I got to Dad's grave I did a thorough search of the whole area; the grave itself, the surrounding gravel, all the hollows in the paths roundabout and down the sides of nearby graves. I even got down on my hands and knees and combed through the little stones. Nothing. Our little gold heart seemed to have disappeared completely.

In the end I sat down beside the grave, closed my eyes and did a meditation.

'Dad,' I said in my mind once I'd become deeply relaxed, 'If you're really there, will you find that little heart for me?'

I carried on breathing deeply, letting the soft air brush my face. Then after about ten minutes I opened my eyes. The cemetery looked just the same. The sun was still shining gently over the gravestones, just as on the day we buried him. I was still alone. Nothing appeared to have changed.

Then something bright on the ground caught my eye. I glanced down and there right by my foot, was the little golden heart. I cried with disbelief as well as joy. Dad had sent it back to me.

A few months later during another visit to the cemetery, I saw something glinting down the side of the grave's edging stone – where nothing had ever glinted before. Crouching down, I carefully prised it out. It was a pendant in the shape of a heart with an angel in the centre. We'd never seen it before and had no idea where it came from but I like to think it was a token from Dad, to show us that though he was with the angels, he still loved us.

I carefully tucked it back where it came from and wedged it in more tightly. It's still there to this day.

And of course as the months and years went by, Mum's condition deteriorated as it was inevitable it would. So one afternoon, my sister and I found ourselves visiting Dad in the cemetery to pray for Mum and then going on to the hospital to visit her.

Afterwards, we walked sadly back to my car, right in the centre of the huge, rapidly emptying hospital car park. From a distance I was slightly alarmed to see there was now something apparently stuck on the windscreen. I sped up anxiously. Surely I couldn't have a parking ticket? I was still inside my allotted time.

But when I reached the car I stopped in amazement. There, right in the centre of the windscreen was, not a parking ticket, but two pieces of perfect white blossom arranged in the shape of a heart.

I glanced round, looking for the tree from which the blossom must have blown. Then I realised what was so odd. There were no trees in the car park. Nor any visible from beyond.

Was this Dad's way of showing us that he was with us and still watching over Mum? I rather think it was.

SIXTEEN:
The view was bathed in a peaceful, angelic light…

And so now, I feel like I've come full circle. I'm still in touch with Simon, we're still friends. I still love to visit the Arthur Findlay College; even though I've accepted I can't be a tutor there, it's still my spiritual home. Even though Mum is no longer a short car journey away, I still talk to her photo every day and tell her how much I miss her.

Yet there is another way our departed loved ones can visit us – and that's in our dreams, when the barrier between our conscious world and the spirit world can sometimes dissolve. Our sleeping minds open wide and once again we can walk and talk with the people we thought we'd lost. 'It was just a dream,' we think when we wake… but how do we know?

One night recently, after I'd been thinking about Mum and feeling sad that she wouldn't be with us on her birthday, I fell asleep as usual but had the most amazing dream – incredibly vivid and detailed.

I found myself in an airy apartment block – I wasn't sure where it was but I could tell it was far away. Mum was with me and she wanted me to help her choose one of the new flats to move into. She was looking so well. Bright-eyed and strong, her lovely hair, thick and shiny the way it used to be.

We stepped forward, opened a door and found ourselves in the most wonderful room, full of light. Opposite, was a huge window overlooking a breathtakingly beautiful scene. I could see a vast blue sea, with sun glittering on the water, and on the horizon, a bright sky merged gently into the waves.

Beside the window was a big door opening onto a spacious balcony, so we wandered outside, and leaned over the balustrade to find a pristine, pale sand beach below.

It so lovely, tears sprang into my eyes. The one thing Mummy loved was being by the sea.

That's why she so enjoyed holidays at our flat in Spain.

This was the place. I knew it. It was tailor-made for Mum.

'This is the one for you Mummy,' I said happily, 'It's perfect - you've always wanted to be by the sea.'

I don't know whether she spoke out loud but she smiled and I knew she agreed.

Just then an old man appeared and he was carrying a huge, leather-bound book with worn, ancient, pages, in his hands. He showed us the book, slowly turning the pages of flowing script and explained to Mum that these were the instructions on how to communicate.

'This book will always be here to help you whenever you need it,' he told her, 'And you'll also be able to communicate through electronic music. You will need to learn this too but help is always here for you.'

Then for some reason, another man come into the flat with his son. The son beckoned me to follow him.

'Mummy I've got to go, I have to do something…' I told her, as I turned to leave, 'I can't stay here. But don't worry it's not far for me to come. I can come back to visit you any time.'

She smiled and nodded serenely. 'I'm happy here,' she said and I could see from the contented glow in her eyes that she meant it.

And then all at once I was back in bed, wide awake, tears streaming down my face.

It felt so real. I was quite sure I'd been privileged to spend a few more precious hours with Mum.

I pushed back the covers and rushed to phone Lorraine. The dream had been so vivid, the colours so strong, I reckoned I'd seen an actual glimpse of Mum's new spirit home.

'That's really odd,' said Lorraine when I'd finished describing what I'd seen, 'because I was looking through some old photos yesterday and I found one I was going to email you. It was Mum on one of her favourite holidays. It sounds very like the place you saw.'

A few minutes later the picture arrived in my inbox.

I could hardly believe my eyes. There was Mum, standing on a balcony staring out over a beautiful blue bay under a sunny, summer sky. The picture lacked the opalescent glow that bathed my dreamscape in such a peaceful, angelic light and yet otherwise, it was incredibly similar.

If Mum could choose where she would like to live in the

spirit world, this was exactly what she'd go for.

And it struck me then – she had indeed learned to communicate. She'd led Lorraine to that particular photograph, and she'd come to me in my sleep, knowing that we would compare notes afterwards. She wanted us to know that she was still around and happy, in her glorious new home.

Above all it proved to me that love never dies. The bonds between you never break. And in the words of the great Doris Stokes: 'You can't die, for the life of you.'

THE END

PS:

Hello there!

Many thanks for reading my book and for getting to the end! I do hope you enjoyed it.

It just occurred to me you might be wondering about my various references to Doris Stokes in these pages.

Well Doris Stokes was a great medium, towards the end of the last century, famous in the Spiritualist community for bringing the movement out of the shadows and into the wider public spotlight. In fact, Doris was once described in the press as the first celebrity medium.

She often visited Stansted Hall, she worked with Gordon Higginson and she wrote a series of her own popular books, still in print and enjoyed to this day. Coincidentally, her book "Voices in my Ear" was the first book I actually read about a medium and I found it totally inspirational.

So imagine my surprise when invited to appear at my first Psychic Fair some years ago, I found myself placed next to a display of Doris Stokes' books, alongside Doris' own ghost-writer, Linda Dearsley who knew her well.

Naturally we had a lot to talk about that afternoon and we ended up becoming friends. So when I decided to write a book of my own, Linda was the ideal person to help me. Sitting on my balcony one sunny afternoon I picked up the phone to call her and as we spoke, a beautiful shimmering dragonfly landed on the third eye of my Buddha head that sits on the corner of the wall. Clearly this was a thumbs up sign from the spirit world to go ahead with the Book.

And ever since then I've often felt Doris at my elbow, urging me on and helping me with my readings. So if you'd like to find out more about what I'm up to now and to keep in touch, come on over to my Website: www.bevmann.co.uk

You're very welcome.

Bev
Mann
x

Linda and I hard at work on the book!

*The dragonfly comes to give a thumbs up
to the book from the spirit world*

PPS:

Oh and finally, before I go...

I would just like to say a big thank you to all the people who've made this book possible.

The idea to write a book about my spiritual journey has been at the back on my mind ever since I had a reading years ago telling me that I will one day write three books! As a person who doesn't read a lot I never imagined it would happen! Amazingly it's come to fruition, thanks to the wonderfully talented Linda Dearsley who I had the privilege to be introduced to by the Spirit World a few years ago. Linda, thank you for your incredible patience throughout the writing of this book and making my dream come true. All those hours spent spinning and knitting this amazing journey together has been so life changing for me. Thank you for your wisdom and keeping me on the straight and narrow!

I would also like to thank my real inspiration for this book – my wonderful family who have loved and nutured me in good times and bad. My courageous mummy and incredible father whom I loved so much. My children, James and Rachel, my reason for living - my love for you both is insurmountable. Thank you for letting me share my story! Then there's my sister Lorraine, always on hand for support, encouragement and dog-sitting! Thank you so much for always being there – you are my best friend and always will be. To Simon, by my side for so long and still a trusted and valued friend, thank you for being part of my journey.

Also, a huge thanks to Keith at MTP Publishing for immediately believing in my book and agreeing to publish it and of course Karolina, the creative genius who put together the magical cover. Plus my friend Mikaela Morgan, the wonderful photographer who put up with me and my sparkly shoes to capture the shot that seemed to sum up this story, unbelievably way before it was even written!

To Nicola Richardson, author of Natural Mystic and former student of mine, thank you for inspiring me to write my book. And to Jester, thank you for your endless support and patience in the last few months of writing it!

To my incredible friends and family, too numerous to mention here but you know who you are… thank you for your loyalty, support, compassion and unconditional friendship over the years – I love you ALL with all my heart.

Last but by no means least, thank you to all the many people I have had the very great pleasure to meet along this journey. To those I have been very honoured to have read for – thank you for trusting me to bring forward your loved ones to make them come alive once more during my readings. I felt your love and watched you smile and cry. You truly touched my heart during those private moments. Thank you for letting me share some of the stories.

To the many students I have taught, mentored, inspired on your own incredible journeys – thank you for trusting me to honour your own pathways. I am truly blessed to be part of your lives too. I hope to be reading your books one day!

And to all those wonderful souls I have yet to meet – I am truly excited!

"The Spirit in me Honours the Spirit in You"

MEET THE AUTHOR:

Bev Mann is a Clairvoyant Spiritual Medium and lives in North West London, UK with a gorgeous bundle of apricot curls - her beloved dog Angel – and not far from her two grown up children. She was born and raised by her loving, traditional Jewish family in Edgware, Middlesex.

She loves shopping, especially for sparkly shoes - and in fact anything glittery! She enjoys long leisurely meals with friends and country walks with Angel.

After many years of mediumship training, Bev also completed a Teacher Training Mentorship programme and has been teaching and running her own workshops and seminars for many years. She has also gone onto teach workshops and development groups in the USA and Europe and is now a Tutor at the Fox Pioneer Centre.

Bev is well known for her compassionate, down to earth approach. Through her work with Spirit, she has become a pioneer of the concept: 'Mediumship from the Heart' – delivering messages with love and empathy so that the client feels their departed loved ones are actually in the room with them.

'Teaching is my passion. I love to help people develop their own unique style of mediumship,' says Bev, 'as a medium, it's a privilege to relay messages of love and guidance from Spirit.

My aim is to show there's only a fine veil between our two worlds and we're still able to communicate with our loved ones in Spirit. Love truly never dies.'

For more information on Bev and her workshops, teaching programmes and readings – check out her website:

www.bevmann.co.uk

and follow Bev here:

www.facebook.com/BevMannMediumPage

www.instagram.com/mediumbevmann

@bevmedium

Spirits, Scandal and Sparkly Shoes

PRIVATE Readings WITH Bev Mann
INTERNATIONAL SPIRITUAL MEDIUM AND TUTOR
IN LONDON OR ONLINE
BEVMANN.CO.UK

SPIRITUAL DEVELOPMENT CLASSES AND PRIVATE MENTORING WITH Bev Mann
INTERNATIONAL SPIRITUAL MEDIUM AND TUTOR
IN LONDON OR ONLINE
BEVMANN.CO.UK

*Available worldwide from
Amazon and all good bookstores*

Michael Terence Publishing

www.mtp.agency

www.facebook.com/mtp.agency

@mtp_agency

Ingram Content Group UK Ltd.
Milton Keynes UK
UKHW020701020523
421098UK00014B/418